# BANGKOK
## ENCOUNTER

**CHINA WILLIAMS**

Bangkok Encounter

**Published by Lonely Planet Publications Pty Ltd**

ABN 36 005 607 983

| | |
|---|---|
| **Australia** | Head Office, Locked Bag 1, Footscray, Vic 3011<br>☎ 03 8379 8000  fax 03 8379 8111<br>talk2us@lonelyplanet.com.au |
| **USA** | 150 Linden St, Oakland, CA 94607<br>☎ 510 893 8555<br>toll free 800 275 8555<br>fax 510 893 8572<br>info@lonelyplanet.com |
| **UK** | 72–82 Rosebery Avenue,<br>Clerkenwell, London EC1R 4RW<br>☎ 020 7841 9000  fax 020 7841 9001<br>go@lonelyplanet.co.uk |

This title was commissioned in Lonely Planet's Melbourne office and produced by: **Commissioning Editors** Jane Thompson, Errol Hunt **Coordinating Editor** Elisa Arduca **Coordinating Cartographer** Anita Banh **Layout Designer** Clara Monitto **Assisting Editor** Margedd Heliosz **Assisting Cartographers** Andy Rojas, Joshua Geoghegan **Managing Editor** Melanie Dankel **Managing Cartographers** David Connolly, Julie Sheridan, Corie Waddell **Cover Designer** Mary Nelson-Parker **Project Manager** Craig Kilburn **Language Content Coordinator** Quentin Frayne **Series Designers** Nic Lehman, Wendy Wright **Thanks to** Sally Darmody, Nicole Hansen, Laura Jane, Katie Lynch, Stephanie Pearson, Suzannah Shwer

ISBN 978 1 74104 570 3

Printed through Colorcraft Ltd, Hong Kong.
Printed in China

**Acknowledgements**

BTS Route Map © 2004 Bangkok Mass Transit System Public Company Limited.

# HOW TO USE THIS BOOK

## Colour-Coding & Maps

Colour-coding is used for symbols on maps an in the text that they relate to (eg all eatin venues on the maps and in the text are give a green fork symbol). Each neighbourhood als gets its own colour, and this is used down th edge of the page and throughout that neigh bourhood section.

Shaded yellow areas on the maps denot 'areas of interest' – for their historical signif cance, their attractive architecture or their grea bars and restaurants. We encourage you to hea to these areas and just start exploring!

## Prices

Multiple prices listed with reviews (eg 70/50 indicates adult/child).

**Send us your feedback** We love to hear from readers – your comments help make our books better. We read every word you send us, and we always guarantee that your feedback goes straight to the appropriate authors. The most useful submissions are rewarded with a free book. To send us your updates and find out about Lonely Planet events, newsletters and travel news visit our award-winning website: *lonelyplanet .com/contact*.

Note: We may edit, reproduce and incorporate your comments in Lonely Planet products such as guidebooks, websites and digital products, so let us know if you don't want your comments reproduced or your name acknowledged. For a copy of our privacy policy visit *lonelyplanet .com/privacy*.

## CHINA WILLIAMS

China grew up in South Carolina, where the hot summers and casual chitchat prepared her well for a Thailand encounter. She first arrived in the kingdom as an English teacher in the provincial capital of Surin and made periodic trips to Bangkok for visa business, navigating the city by public bus long before the Skytrain was anything more than a stalled eyesore. China now lives in the US, skipping across the Pacific twice a year to Thailand to update various guidebooks. Home is most recently in Montana with her husband, Matt, and son, Felix.

## CHINA'S THANKS

Thanks to my usual Bangkok crowd: Mason and Jane, the staff at *Bangkok 101*, Clay and Jessica, Sarah Wintle, Austin Bush, Fawn, Ruengsang and the international team at the TAT headquarters. More thanks to Matt for all the arty video messages, and baby son Felix who announced his arrival *in utero* on this trip. Thanks also to Jane Thompson and the Lonely Planet production team.

## CONTRIBUTING AUTHOR & PHOTOGRAPHER

After graduating from the University of Oregon, Austin Bush received a scholarship to study Thai and has remained in Thailand ever since. After several years at a stable job, he decided to pursue a career as a freelance photographer/writer. This has taken him as far as northern Pakistan, and as near as Bangkok's Aw Taw Kaw Market (p144), and will hopefully compensate him financially at some point.

**Our Readers** Many thanks to the travellers who wrote to us with helpful hints, useful advice and interesting anecdotes. Eileen Hairel, Prapanporn Hoono, Nabeel Ibrahim, Ramkumar Singh, Nattaporn Pongthep.

**Cover photograph** Barbecued fish for sale at a street market, Jerry Alexander/LPI. **Internal photographs** p49, p78, p86, p101, p147 by Austin Bush; All other photographs by Lonely Planet Images and by Greg Elms except p8, p16, p17, p20, p29, p31, p32, p68, p70, p104, p112, p124, p127, p128, p135, p149, p157, p164, p170, p172, p173 Richard I'Anson; p21, p26, p34, p64 Mick Elmore; p152, p158 Richard Nebesky; p13 Tom Cockrem; p151 Lee Foster; p30 Kraig Lieb; p33 Andrew Lubran; p154 Craig Pershouse.
All images are copyright of the photographers unless otherwise indicated. Many of the images in this guide are available for licensing from **Lonely Planet Images:** www.lonelyplanetimages.com.

A meditative stroll through the streets of bustling Ko Ratanakosin (p44)

# CONTENTS

# THIS IS BANGKOK

Bangkok is excess in all of its unrestrained glory. Bigger, better, more: the city is insatiable, a monster that feeds on concrete, shopping malls and diesel exhaust.

The city demands that you be in the present and in the moment, not necessarily for a religious epiphany, but because the city is self-absorbed and superficial, blissfully free of wrinkle-inducing self-reflection. Smiles and *sànùk* (the Thai word for 'fun') are the key passports into Bangkok society. A compliment here, a joke there – the demands of social lubrication in this megalopolis are more akin to a small village than an anonymous city and a necessity for survival.

As Bangkok forcefully kneads out of you all demands for order and predictability, you'll understand the famous Thai smile. It is the metaphorical brakes on the urban overdrive. Packed into these concrete corridors are religious spectacle, unapologetic consumerism and multi-flavoured hedonism – corrupting and purifying souls within footsteps of each other. A tragicomic confluence of human desires and aspirations best viewed through a detached smile.

Of the famous and infamous attractions, Bangkok's best feature is its intermingling of opposites. A modern world of affluence orbits around a serene traditional core. Step outside the four-star hotels into a typical Siamese village where taxi drivers knock back energy drinks and upcountry transplants grill chicken on a streetside barbecue. Hop the Skytrain to the glitzy shopping malls where trust-fund babies examine luxury brands as carefully as the housewives inspect produce at the open-air markets. Or appreciate the attempts at enlightenment at the city's famous temples, doorstep shrines, or simple acts of kindness amid the urban bustle.

You can jump between all of these worlds – wining and hobnobbing at a chic club, eating at a streetside market, getting plucked and pummelled into something more beautiful, or sweating profusely on a long unplanned march. Bangkok is an urban connoisseur's dream come true.

**Top** An imposing welcome at the entrance to the National Theatre (p52), Ko Ratanakosin **Bottom left** Funky protection ware: amulets for all Thais **Bottom right** Take your pick at the streetside markets on Th Samsen, Thewet (p66)

>HIGHLIGHTS

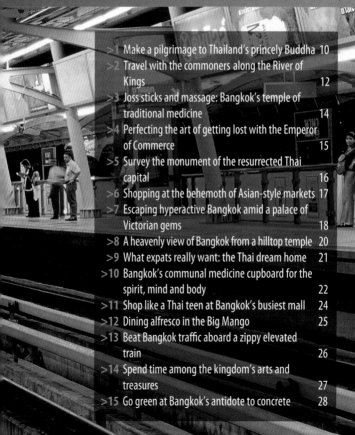

Get there in a flash on the Skytrain (p26)

# >1 GRAND PALACE & WAT PHRA KAEW

## MAKE A PILGRIMAGE TO THAILAND'S PRINCELY BUDDHA

Wat Phra Kaew (p46) is an elaborate and colourful temple that easily distracts first-time visitors from the namesake figure: the Emerald Buddha, a diminutive statue carved of nephrite (a type of jade, not emerald) housed in the main hall. This is one of the most revered of the Thai Buddhas, representing the legitimacy of the reigning dynasty and claiming a swashbuckler's history. The dazzling figure was discovered in northern Thailand in the 15th century when a stupa was split open by lightning. To conceal its lustre the figure was covered in plaster (a common practice during the days of wars and bandits). Succeeding generations eventually forgot what the plaster hid inside until an accidental fall revealed the contents. In the mid-16th century, Laotian invaders stole the sacred Buddha but the Thais retrieved it in battle and used it to bestow divine approval on General Taksin who assumed the throne after the fall of Ayuthaya. The figure was placed in its present location during the reign of Rama I (King Buddha Yodfa; r 1782–1809),

### AN EPIC CHALLENGE: THE RAMAKIAN

In the corners of Wat Phra Kaew are murals of the *Ramakian* story, the Thai version of the Indian epic *Ramayana*. The tale unfolds clockwise from the northern gate and each frame depicts the main event in the centre with the conclusion depicted either above or below.

The story begins with the hero, Rama (the green-faced character), and his bride Sita (the beautiful topless maiden). The young couple are banished to the forest, along with Rama's brother. In this pastoral setting, the evil king Ravana (the character with many arms and faces) disguises himself as a hermit in order to kidnap Sita.

Rama joins forces with Hanuman, the monkey king (logically depicted as the white monkey), to attack Ravana and rescue Sita. Although Rama has the pedigree, Hanuman is the unsung hero. He is loyal, fierce and clever. En route to the final fairy-tale ending, great battles and schemes of trickery ensue until Ravana is finally killed. After withstanding a loyalty test of fire, Sita and Rama are triumphantly reunited.

the first king in the Chakri dynasty, when the capital was moved across the river from Thonburi to Bangkok in 1782.

Because of its royal status, the Emerald Buddha is ceremoniously draped in monastic robes, which are changed every season (hot, wet, and cool) by the king himself.

Next door to Wat Phra Kaew is the Grand Palace (p46), a vast compound where successive kings, their families and attendants lived until Rama V (King Chulalongkorn; r 1868–1910) moved the royal seat to what is now known as Dusit Palace Park (p18). The primary buildings display a fusion of Thai and Western architectural styles and are occasionally used for official functions, but the formal grounds lack the vibrancy of the neighbouring temple.

A strict dress code is enforced at the temple; see p46 for guidelines and more information.

# >2 MAE NAM CHAO PHRAYA

## TRAVEL WITH THE COMMONERS ALONG THE RIVER OF KINGS

Central Thais are river people, building their homes, livelihoods and capitals along the waterways. One such artery is the Mae Nam Chao Phraya (literally the 'River of Kings'), which starts in the mountains of northern Thailand, sweeps past the former capital of Ayuthaya and defines the western boundary of Bangkok before it reaches the Gulf of Thailand some 370km away from its source.

The river is always teeming with activity: hulking freighter boats trail behind dedicated tugs, elegant long-tail boats skip across the wake, and children practice cannonballs into the muddy water. The residents claiming a waterfront view range from world-class hotels to sweaty warehouses and auspicious temples. As evening sets in, cool river breezes mellow the harsh temperatures and the blinding sun slips into serene streaks of reds and golds. From this vantage point, sooty Bangkok suddenly looks beautiful.

The best way to explore the watery side of Bangkok is aboard the river express boat (p200), which sprints from Wat Ratchasingkhon in the south of the city to Nonthaburi in the north. At docks along the way, the ferry discharges crowds of map-toting tourists, commuting office clerks and groups of monks. (The back of the starboard-side is reserved for monks; women should opt for the port-side.)

### LONG-TAIL SAFARI

Glimpses of the days when the city was wired by water rather than asphalt still survive along the canals (khlong) that crisscross Thonburi. One of the largest is Khlong Bangkok Noi, which is lined with stilt homes that use the canal as everything, including the kitchen sink. This waterway was actually the original course of the Mae Nam Chao Phraya but it was bypassed in the 16th century to ease navigation to Ayuthaya.

Climb aboard a hired long-tail boat to zip into these aquatic neighbourhoods. Boat hires are available at all piers on the Bangkok side of the river. Some charge by the boat (700B per hour), others per person (200B to 300B per person). Canal sightseeing tours that include Wat Arun or other riverside attractions are best suited for large groups instead of more agile types.

Start an upriver journey from Tha Sathon, accessible via the Skytrain Saphan Taksin station. On your right is the old *faràng* (Westerner) quarter – what we refer to as Riverside – first inhabited by seafarers and multinational shipping companies. The Oriental Hotel and other neoclassical buildings are a few of the remaining memorials to this era when the water was the main thoroughfare.

Around Tha Ratchawong, the river brushes up against Chinatown (p15) and its cubby-holed warehouses where goods are unloaded the old-fashioned way – by hand.

After a while, striking Wat Arun (p16) looms on your left and then ornate Grand Palace and Wat Phra Kaew (p10) on your right – forming a triangular convergence of sacred sites.

North of Saphan Phra Ram VIII, an elegant suspension bridge, the concrete dissipates into greenery and sunburned temples. The final stop is Nonthaburi, the launching point for boat trips to sleepy Ko Kret (p156).

# >3 WAT PHO

## JOSS STICKS AND MASSAGE: BANGKOK'S TEMPLE OF TRADITIONAL MEDICINE

Wat Phra Kaew gets all the spotlight, but Wat Pho is everyone's favourite. Rarely crowded, the rambling grounds of Wat Pho (p50) claim a 16th-century birthday, pre-dating the city itself. It is also the country's biggest temple. Still not impressed? How about Wat Pho's primary Buddha – a reclining figure that nearly dwarfs its sizable shelter. Symbolic of Buddha's death and passage into nirvana, the reclining Buddha measures 46m and is gilded with gold leaf. Lining the soles of the feet is a magnificent mother-of-pearl inlay depicting the 108 auspicious *láksànà* (traits) that signify the birth of a pre-destined Buddha.

During the reign pf Rama III (King Nang Klao; r 1824–51), Wat Pho was dedicated as an open university and continues to serve as the national headquarters for the teaching and preservation of traditional Thai medicine and massage. On the temple grounds, there are un-air-conditioned massage pavilions (see p53), while the training school is nearby with air-con rooms.

The granite giants that decorate the courtyard of Wat Pho are perhaps Thailand's oldest immigrants. These statues arrived aboard Chinese ships as ballasts in the empty hulls and were left behind on the return trip. Some are warriors, others philosophers and one is said to be Marco Polo. Other statuary includes visual teaching tools such as the hill of hermits depicting different healing yogic poses.

## >4 CHINATOWN

**PERFECTING THE ART OF GETTING LOST WITH THE EMPEROR OF COMMERCE**

Chinatown (p72) is pure energy bundled into blazing neon signs, belching buses and full-on commerce. Each block specialises in a certain product: rubber bathplugs here, guns and ammo there, painted signs and coffins. Not much is souvenir-worthy but all of this small-scale industry in one place is rarer these days than bound feet.

The main artery, Th Yaowarat, lends its name to the district and is crowded with gold shops – sealed glass-front buildings looking more like Chinese altars than downtown jewellers. Wat Mangkon Kamalawat (p75) venerates both Chinese and Thai deities. Another revered temple is Wat Traimit (p75), famous for its golden Buddha.

There's more life behind the cacophonous arteries. Sampeng Lane (p77) is now a wholesale market, but it used to be a red-light district.

Trok Itsaranuphap (p75) is the shortest, greatest stroll in the city; the alley begins near Talat Gao (Old Market), which claims mythic longevity, and eventually leads to stalls selling ritual offerings for the deceased. Tucked behind River City shopping centre, the area known as Talat Noi (between Th Songwat and Th Si Phraya) is a labyrinth of machine repair shops and pencil-thin footpaths.

HIGHLIGHTS

## >5 WAT ARUN

### SURVEY THE MONUMENT OF THE RESURRECTED THAI CAPITAL

Standing sentry along the Mae Nam Chao Phraya river bank, Wat Arun (p48) commands as much visual respect as its history would demand. It was here, on the Thonburi side of the river, that General Taksin resurrected the Thai capital after the fall of Ayuthaya. What was then a local shrine was transformed into the seat of power. But, alas, the Temple of Dawn (so named for Taksin's literal and metaphoric arrival in 1767) lost its bid for monarchical monogamy with the crowning of a new king and a new capital across the river in Bangkok.

What stands today retains a sense of martial superiority with a towering phallic-shaped stupa that rises to a height of 82m and mimics the aggressive architectural style of Angkor Wat. This central tower is symbolic of Mt Meru, centre of the universe in Hindu and Buddhist mythology. Some argue that Wat Arun is more stunning from a distance, but a close-up reveals a colourful floral-motif mosaic of porcelain, once used as ballast in Chinese sailing ships. A flight of steep stairs is open to the public for better views of the tiered layer's decorative Hindu figures: the *kinnari* (half human-half bird) and Indra (god of the sky) astride Erawan (Indra's elephant mount). A pair of *yaksha* (giants) stand guard at the main chapel, and Phra Pai, the god of wind, is frozen on his horse in the minor *prang* (corn-cob-shaped stupa).

# >6 CHATUCHAK WEEKEND MARKET

**SHOPPING AT THE BEHEMOTH OF ASIAN-STYLE MARKETS**

A rambling flea market of bargains, Chatuchak Weekend Market (p143) is Bangkok's biggest and most intense market. Imagine supersizing the average Thai market with its narrow passageways lined with merchandise, and you've got a close approximation of Chatuchak. Silks, extra-small fashions, fighting cocks and fighting fish, fluffy puppies, and souvenirs for the insatiable *faràng* – if it can be sold in Thailand, you'll find it here. From everyday to clubby, clothes dominate most of the market, where young designers unveil their wares. Look out for second-hand clothes that have obviously emigrated from Western closets.

Your wallet may already be champing at the bit, but go prepared and go early as there are hundreds of thousands of visitors per day, crowding and sweating in the precious open spaces. In theory, Chatuchak is organised into logical, numbered sections but good luck trying to decipher this while pointy elbows nudge you along. Do some reconnaissance work with Nancy Chandler's *Map of Bangkok*, available at English-language book shops such as Asia Books (p83).

Be warned that there's no air-conditioning and you'll likely suffer extreme claustrophobia. If dehydration sets in, head towards the clock tower where there is a concentration of cafés or duck outside for a refreshing bowl of *khànŏm jiin* (rice noodles with curry sauce). In the evenings, local musicians serenade the crowds who are capping off their shopping spree with happy hour.

HIGHLIGHTS

# >7 DUSIT PALACE PARK

## ESCAPING HYPERACTIVE BANGKOK AMID A PALACE OF VICTORIAN GEMS

No other spot in Bangkok is as pretty and peaceful as Dusit Palace Park (p69), a three-dimensional scrapbook made by Rama V of his European tour. Ushering in a new millennium, Rama V moved the royal residence from the ancient confines of the Grand Palace to this European-inspired complex, which is now open to the public and filled with museums honouring the former king and Thai cultural traditions. Beyond its historical attributes, Dusit Palace is a much-needed respite from Bangkok's teeming energy.

The most famous palace building is the enormous golden-teak mansion, Vimanmek Teak Palace (p70), which was used by the king and his wife, children and concubines as their primary home. Vimanmek Teak Palace's 81 rooms are elegant and overwhelmingly pastel. But the highlight, besides the architecture, is seeing Rama V's personal effects and antiques – among them, grand pianos, Ching dynasty pieces and the first menu in Thailand – and getting an insight into how the royals lived.

Reflecting the king's ingenious use of Western influences, Abhisek Dusit Throne Hall (p68) is a tasteful mélange of Moorish and Victorian influences with a distinctly Thai character. Today the hall is used to exhibit a collection of regional handicrafts.

Near the Th Ratchawithi entrance, two residence halls display the HM King Bhumibol Photography Exhibitions, collections of photographs and paintings by the present monarch. Among many loving photos of his wife and children are also historic pictures of the king playing the clarinet with Benny Goodman and Louis Armstrong in 1960. Further

## TRADITIONAL DANCE

Forget the canned dinner theatres with Thai dancing and dull dishes. Free daily performances of traditional dance are held at 10.30am and 2pm beside the Vimanmek Teak Palace. In this relaxed setting, you'll see several authentic dances from the different regions of Thailand without feeling like a captive tourist.

along is the Ancient Cloth Museum (p68) and tucked away beside the Th U-Thong exit is the Royal Thai Elephant Museum (p69).

The domed neoclassical building at the foot of Royal Plaza is Ananta Samakhom Throne Hall, built in the early 1900s by Italian architects in the style of European government houses. Used today for ceremonial purposes, the throne hall also hosted the first meeting of the Thai parliament until their meeting place was moved to a facility nearby. Visitors can explore the architecture of the building and view rotating exhibits.

Because Dusit Park is royal property, visitors must dress appropriately (long pants or skirts, and shirts with sleeves); sarongs are available if your lower half isn't covered enough.

# >8 WAT SAKET & GOLDEN MOUNT

**A HEAVENLY VIEW OF BANGKOK FROM A HILLTOP TEMPLE**

Bangkok is a city of views: skyscrapers gaze out upon an ocean of towers. But few buildings survey the old city from the 360-degree vantage point of Wat Saket (p57). From the top of the temple's artificial hill, called the Golden Mount, Bangkok is transformed into a breezy village of terracotta-roofed temples not yet inhabited by concrete towers. As is the custom, a portion of the ashes of deceased benefactors are built into the temple, in this case the plaques are planted into the side of the hill along with lush greenery. Near the top, a row of brass bells are rung by the faithful before they reach the golden *chedi* that caps the top. There are a handful of explanations for ringing the bells: some say they are sending messages to heaven, others to chase away evil spirits, but all agree that good luck factors in it somehow.

The hill itself was originally intended to form the body of a giant *chedi,* commissioned by Rama III, but it collapsed due to its soft soil base. Rama IV (King Mongkut; r 1851–68) resumed the construction project by building a small golden *chedi* on its crest. Until the 1960s, Golden Mount was the tallest point in Bangkok – a title since ceded to a grove of skyscrapers.

At the base of the Golden Mount, you'll find demure Wat Saket, which was built during the time of Rama I and serves more of an everyday religious function than a tourist attraction.

# >9 JIM THOMPSON'S HOUSE

**WHAT EXPATS REALLY WANT: THE THAI DREAM HOME**

Every foreign visitor who pads around Jim Thompson's House (p82) secretly wishes to live here for a day or more. The former resident was one of Bangkok's most famous expats and used his home as a repository for ageing Thai traditions and artwork. As old wooden houses were falling derelict, Thompson salvaged six teak houses (reputedly built without nails) and assembled them on the banks of Khlong Saen Saeb on an astrologically auspicious date in 1959.

The rooms are adorned with his art collection and personal possessions, including rare Chinese porcelain pieces and Burmese, Cambodian and Thai artefacts, and the tropical garden is punctuated by lush plantings and lotus ponds.

American-born Thompson was an intriguing chap in both life and death. He served in Thailand during WWII and soon returned to Bangkok after finding his hometown of New York City a tad too quiet. During his tenure in the City of Angels (as Bangkok is known), he helped revive the Thai cottage industry of handwoven silk, a tradition losing favour domestically. He sent samples of his neighbours' textiles to European fashion houses, resulting in a silk business that continues to this day. His charmed life came to a dramatic end when he vanished during an afternoon stroll in Malaysia's Cameron Highlands in 1967.

# >10 WAT MAHATHAT & AMULET MARKET

## BANGKOK'S COMMUNAL MEDICINE CUPBOARD FOR THE SPIRIT, MIND AND BODY

Most tourists skip the area north of Wat Phra Kaew eager to tick off more famous attractions elsewhere, but no where in this conflicted city is the daily practice of Thai Buddhism more alive than in the crowded corridors around Wat Mahathat (p48). All aspects of the religion – from the sacred study of scripture and daily meditation to the folk beliefs in lucky charms – are modestly on display for the cultural wanderer.

Rambling Wat Mahathat is the most important centre of Buddhist learning in Southeast Asia because of the Buddhist university on the site, Mahathat Rajavidyalaya, which educates monks from Laos, Cambodia and Vietnam and is the national centre of the Mahanikai monastic sect (one of the two sects that make up the Sangha, or Buddhist brotherhood, in Thailand). Wat Mahathat was built in the Ayuthaya period, but very little of it appears historically striking; its attraction is its role in the community with daily comings and goings of laity and monks. Lots of foreigners wander onto the grounds looking for the daily meditation courses (p53) and the resident English-speaking monks make enthusiastic guides.

Outside the temple gates on Th Maharat is a daily Amulet Market (p50; *tàlàat phrá khrêuang*) selling wearable protection from evil spirits or bad fortune. The market has the ambience of a flea market

### TAKING THE CURE

Along Th Maharat are closet-sized shops that sell traditional Thai medicines, typically made of herbs and employing the philosophies of Ayurvedic and Chinese healing traditions. Commercial formulas sold at these shops contain ingredients you're more likely to meet in a Thai curry: galangal and lemongrass, which can treat everything from bad breath to stomach ulcers. Most products are labelled only in Thai, but the **Royal Bee Herbal Shop** ( ☎ 0 1614 8477; 376 Th Maharat), across from Wat Pho, has handy English translations.

but the collections are as highly prized as rare antiques. Most of the amulets are square-shaped medallions embossed with images of Buddha, Hindu deities or famous monks, and carry with them protective powers to stop bullets, ensure fertility or reap material success. Thais working in high-risk professions, such as cab drivers and construction workers, are some of the most reliable amulet buyers as these holy images are more trusted than Western-style insurance policies. But it is rare to meet a Bangkok Thai who doesn't wear some type of amulet for general wellbeing.

Being so close to Thammasat University, the market also caters to student needs as well. Alongside a bin of Buddha amulets are stores selling graduation cap and gowns and further back along the river are squatty student-cheap restaurants that sneak a peek of the river.

## >11 MAH BOON KRONG

**SHOP LIKE A THAI TEEN AT BANGKOK'S BUSIEST MALL**

Forget everything you know about shopping malls and prepare to be wowed by Mah Boon Krong, nicknamed MBK (p85). Nearly all of the city's population under 20 can be found here on a more regular basis than they can in class or at home. It's the social nexus of the city with down-to-earth market sensibilities and refreshing air-conditioning.

MBK's main event is the people-watching: grandmas step nervously onto the escalators and hip teenagers cluster into tight cliques. Need a custom-made girdle, mantelpiece painting of you and your dog, or what about some name cards? Probably not, but these are strapping businesses in MBK.

There are of course many irresistible tourist bargains in this everyman mall. Contact lenses, mobile phones and cut-rate fashions are primary draws, along with every permutation of fast-food franchise. Even though it's a Pizza Hut, it's still a distinctly Thai experience: Thais put ketchup on their pizza, and KFC recently invented their own version of East-West fusion with 'cheezy fries', French fries dipped in melted cheese and then puffed rice (surprisingly delicious).

No visit to MBK is complete without sucking down some sugary drinks, picking up some new zits and catching a movie at the top floor cinema. This is the Thai teen life you never had.

# >12 FOOD MARKETS & STREET STALLS

## DINING ALFRESCO IN THE BIG MANGO

Bangkok's reputation as one of the most polluted cities in the world belies its forte as an outdoor dining capital. Despite the modern conveniences of air-conditioning and fashion cafés, the best meals in the city also called the Big Mango are still the tried-and-true markets and food stalls that make it possible to nibble the day away. Forget about three square meals, when in Bangkok, locals snack throughout the day, packing away at least four meals before sunset.

Like a sundial, the sidewalk landscape of food stalls is an approximate indication of the time of day. In the mornings, vendors sell steaming cups of thick filtered coffee sweetened with condensed milk or mini baton-shaped doughnuts dunked in glasses of warm soy milk. By midday the buffet has switched to premade rice and curries, made-to-order rice dishes and fruit snacks. Once the traffic and the heat subsides (relatively speaking), the dining social hour begins, with sleepy lanes being converted into communal dinner tables. Friends gather around plastic tables slurping down shared dishes or bowls of noodles chased with bottles of beer or fruit juices. Perhaps no other dining experience will leave such a lasting impression as an alfresco meal complete with a spice-induced sweat moustache.

Vendor carts can be found in every nook and cranny of the city. Popular food markets include Aw Taw Kaw (p144), Soi 38 Night Market (p133) and Chinatown Market.

## >13 SKYTRAIN

**BEAT BANGKOK TRAFFIC ABOARD A ZIPPY ELEVATED TRAIN**

In a perpetually gridlocked city, there's an escape away from Bangkok's ground-level clog: the Skytrain, one of the world's slickest mass-transit systems. The Skytrain glides high above the city streets connecting the various tentacles of new Bangkok. From this elevated viewpoint, you can peer into an antlike construction site or the garden compounds of the city elite. You can also hop from Siam Square to Sathon in 10 minutes during rush hour, a science-fiction fantasy in the pre-Skytrain days.

Although its coverage is limited, the Skytrain has transformed the horizontal mobility of the upwardly mobile, whisking them from one shopping mall to another without ever having to step down to ground level. A rough count reveals at least half a dozen shopping malls directly connected to various Skytrain stations.

Besides its practical, if elite, uses, the Skytrain provides a necessary introduction to modern Bangkok. The old city gets all the attention from the tourist brochures, but the new city is the urban equivalent of the kid's table at a family gathering: rowdier and more fun. The open-air stations are crowded with Japanese-pop aesthetics: blaring advertisements, funky fashion, and a barrage of ringing mobile phones. A great break from temple fatigue.

# > 14 NATIONAL MUSEUM

## SPEND TIME AMONG THE KINGDOM'S ARTS AND TREASURES

If the National Museum (p47) were a person, it would be a scatter-brained yet brilliant university lecturer. Why? Its collections are top-rate but haphazardly arranged, lacking the usual museum teaching tools.

Occupying an 18th-century palace, the National Museum contains exhaustive collections of Thai and Southeast Asian art and artefacts. A navigational map is issued at the ticket booth, but in order to really understand the importance and context of the exhibits a guided tour is necessary. Tours focus primarily on the art wing, which spans the development of religious sculpture from Dvaravati to Ayuthaya style.

The Gallery of Thai History has computer terminals and audio explanations providing a chronological tour through Thai history. For the look-and-nod types, check out the elaborate funeral chariots that have carried the ashes of royalty. Room 15 offers insights into the benefits of migration, displaying the musical instruments of a Phat Mon ensemble, introduced by the Mon people (one of the earliest ethnic groups in Southeast Asia). The money collection exhibits fat Sukhothai coins said to have magical properties and the long *hoi* money used in the north. Visit the restored Buddhaisawan (Phutthaisawan) Chapel to see one of Thailand's revered Buddha images, Phra Phuttha Sihing.

## >15 LUMPHINI PARK

### GO GREEN AT BANGKOK'S ANTIDOTE TO CONCRETE

Does jet lag have you up at the crack of dawn? Instead of tossing and turning in bed, get down to Lumphini Park (p114) for a morning workout. Around 7am is when the pathways are crammed with people gliding into t'ai chi poses or kicking up their heels at aerobics classes. Groups of the elderly settle under trees for open-air karaoke sessions. The vendors carefully arrange their stalls of snake blood and bile, popular health tonics. Joggers pound their way around the park. And then it all stops, suddenly, when the national anthem is played at 8am. (If you're still here, remember to come to a standstill until the anthem is completed.) On weekends, beefcakes colonise the weights corner and *tàkrâw* players turn the game of volleyball into a football match.

Lumphini Park is named after Buddha's birthplace in Nepal and provides the best free entertainment in town – even more so during the concert performances in the cool months or in kite-flying season, when there are dashing antics in the skies above. For a nominal charge, you can hire one of the paddleboats that putter around the enormous ornamental lake. But you don't need to part with any money in order to experience the feeling that you've escaped from the big smoke, if only for a moment.

# >BANGKOK DIARY

There's always something going on in Bangkok – be it an international festival sponsored by the foreign cultural centres or a national holiday honouring the monarchy. In addition to the cultural and religious events listed here, the city's galleries host opening exhibition parties and Bangkok's bars and restaurants have adopted any foreign holiday that requires a celebratory drink. The city celebrates no less than three New Year's (International, Thai and Chinese). Check the websites of TAT (www.tourismthailand.org) or Bangkok Tourist Division (www.bangkoktourist.com) for festival dates as they vary. Also check the monthly magazine *Bangkok 101* for city events.

A Thai celebration isn't complete without traditional dancing, this time at Erawan Shrine (p82)

BANGKOK DIARY

Decked out to ring in Chinese New Year

# JANUARY

## Bangkok International Film Festival

www.bangkokfilm.org

Homegrown talent and overseas indies flicker on the silver screen of Bangkok's cinemas during this 10-day festival. Occasionally this festival is celebrated in February.

# FEBRUARY

## Chinese New Year

Thai-Chinese celebrate the lunar New Year, with house cleaning, lion dances and fireworks in Chinatown (pictured above). Occasionally this holiday occurs in March.

# MARCH

## Kite-Flying Season

The skies over Sanam Luang (Royal Field) are filled with colourful, animal-shaped kites during this windy month.

## Bangkok International Art Festival

www.bkkartfest.com

Local and international artists working in such unconventional mediums as graffiti and street art get showcased at the city's hip venues. Bangkok isn't the edgiest town for such bizarre doodles but the younger generation is showing more angst.

# APRIL

## Songkhran

Bangkok's wildest festival, Songkhran is a celebration of the Thai lunar New Year involving water throwing. Once a subdued affair, the celebration has devolved into a citywide water fight. Foreigners, especially well-dressed ones, are obvious targets for mischievous locals. The majority of the mayhem occurs on Th Khao San.

# MAY

## Royal Ploughing Ceremony

His Majesty the King commences rice-planting season with a Brahmin ritual held at Sanam Luang. Ancient costumes, sacred oxen and the royal plough star in the event.

## Visakha Bucha

Buddha's birth, enlightenment and passing away are honoured with candlelit processions and other merit-making activities on this religious holiday. Wat Benchamabophit (p71) is well-known for its evening rituals.

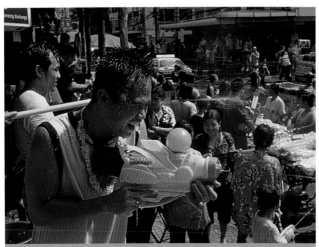

If you can't beat 'em, join 'em. Passers-by targeted by water pistol–wielding revellers during Songkhran

All smiles during a traditional dance performance at Vimanmek Palace (p70)

# JUNE

## International Festival of Music & Dance (Part I)

www.bangkokfestivals.com

Arts and culture performances are sponsored by the Thailand Cultural Centre. Part II of the festival continues in September.

# JULY

## Khao Phansa

This marks the beginning of the wet season and the start of Buddhist Lent, when young men enter the monkhood. This is a lunar holiday, so dates vary.

# AUGUST

## HM Queen's Birthday

The queen's birthday (August 12) is celebrated throughout the country. Many royalists wear blue (the colour associated with the day of the week of the queen's birth) to show respect. This day is also recognised as Mother's Day.

# SEPTEMBER

## International Festival of Music & Dance (Part II)

www.bangkokfestivals.com

The second instalment of this performing arts festival spotlights opera, ballet and folk traditions from around the world.

# OCTOBER

## King Chulalongkorn Day

On the anniversary of his death Rama V is honoured with a celebration – large crowds 'make merit' in front of the equestrian statue of him at Royal Plaza.

## Vegetarian Festival

This 10-day Chinese-Buddhist festival requires the devout to purify minds and bodies by abstaining from meat. It is primarily observed in Chinatown with vendors preparing meatless meals. Just look for the yellow banners to denote vegetarian observation.

## Ork Phansa

This marks the end of the wet season and Buddhist Lent. Buddhists typically attend temples to listen to sermons and to promenade around the temple three times.

# NOVEMBER

## Loi Krathong

Thailand's most striking festival, Loi Krathong honours the guardian spirit of water with small lotus-shaped boats containing a lit candle that are set adrift on Mae Nam Chao Phraya or other water sources. It is said that couples who float a *kràthong* (ceremonial float) together will never drift apart. Because this is a lunar festival, sometimes it falls in October.

## Wat Saket Temple Fair

A good old-fashioned temple fair – part religious, part carnival – is held on the grounds of Wat Saket. A candlelit procession climbs to the top of the Golden Mount, while food and trinket vendors occupy the temple grounds.

## Bangkok's Pride Parade

www.utopia-asia.com

A week-long gay pride festival culminates in a parade of floats and costumes on Th Silom.

Fire for the guardian spirit of water, Loi Krathong

BANGKOK DIARY

It's my party: the king surveys the honour guard at his birthday parade

# DECEMBER

## HM King's Birthday

The country's revered monarchy is honoured on the king's birthday (5 December) with household decorations and twinkling lights around Bangkok's Grand Palace. This day is also recognised as 'Father's Day' and provides many city workers an opportunity to travel home to the provinces.

## Bangkok Jazz Fest

www.bangkokjazzfestival.com
A three-night musical event of jazz is held outdoors at Dusit Palace Park. International and local talent serenade the lounging audience.

## New Year's Eve

Fireworks and festivities take place across the city in honour of the international new year.

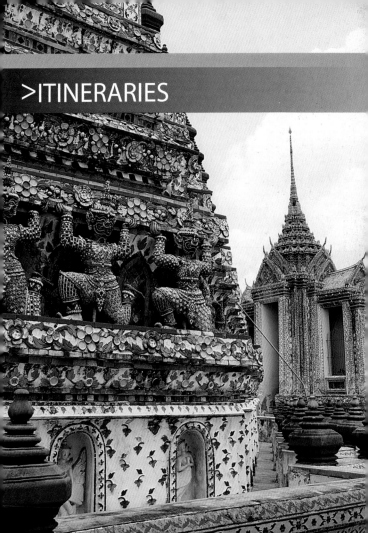

# >ITINERARIES

The monumental beauty of Wat Arun (p48) never ceases to amaze

# ITINERARIES

Just getting around Bangkok is a mental and physical workout. The heat and humidity is withering, and the city layout confounding. Be flexible with your expectations and leave lots of room for snacking and wandering. During these unplanned outings, you'll stumble upon Bangkok's best sights: kids playing badminton, corner gossip sessions and open-air kitchens.

## DAY ONE

Get up early in the morning to watch the silent promenade of monks on their alms route, collecting the day's sustenance from housewives and shopkeepers. Banglamphu is the best neighbourhood to watch this daily ritual. Then head over to the Grand Palace & Wat Phra Kaew (p10) before the day gets too hot and the crowds too thick. Afterwards, stroll over to neighbouring Wat Pho (p14) and hop across the river to Wat Arun (p16). That's enough temple-spotting for one day. Catch a river express boat back to Banglamphu for lunch at Ton Pho (p63) and wander along Th Phra Athit and into the backpackers ghetto around Th Khao San. Sup at Khrua Nopparat (p61) and imbibe at the streetside bars on Th Khao San (p63).

## DAY TWO

If you're primed for more heat and crowds, head to Chinatown (p15) and wander the fresh food and hardware markets for shopping voyeurism. Stop into the various temples or just poke around the streamlike *soi* that will render you thoroughly lost – the only way to explore this neighbourhood. Afterward you'll need a sensory soother with a visit to peaceful Jim Thompson's House (p21), a tranquil collection of antique architecture and art. If you're a glutton for punishment or just a glutton for good food, return to Chinatown once the sun sets for a streetside seafood feast on Soi Texas (p79). Wrap up the evening with a night cap at a sky-high bar (see p109) that drinks in the twinkling lights and ambient roar of the city below.

## DAY THREE

If it's a weekend, take the Skytrain all the way to the last stop to the mammoth Chatuchak Weekend Market (p17), which will consume a whole day

**Top left** Dusit Park's Royal Plaza (p19) is the place to express your monarchical devotion **Top right** Need a one-stop shop for all of life's little luxuries? Try Siam Paragon (p89) **Bottom** Kicking back in Sukhumvit's cafés (p129)

with shopping, bargaining and sweating. Combat the heat with lots of treats at the market's makeshift cafés. Arrive early in the morning to beat the heat and the crowds and give yourself a late-day siesta. Then head out to catch some down-home food and music at Vientiane Kitchen (p133), a barn-like restaurant of northeastern-style Thai food and good times. After searing your taste buds with the famously spicy cuisine, polish off the night with a visit to some of Bangkok's international-strength clubs, such as Bed Supperclub (p135), Q Bar (p136) or Santika (p146). The crowds are fickle at this late-night playgrounds so watch the press – try the Bangkok Recorder (www.bangkokrecorder.com) – for visiting DJs or popular theme nights.

## BANGKOK HAVEN

Whether pouring rain or boiling hot, Bangkok is sometimes best viewed from inside an air-conditioned building. If you've landed during the wet season, keep in mind that the monsoons usually strike in the late afternoon and can make catching a cab almost impossible. Seek shelter in the comfortable cocoon of the city's various shopping centres. For a city that resists planning, the shopping centres have managed to proliferate around Siam Square and have spread into covered walkways leading directly to the Skytrain stations so that fragile fashionistas are protected from the elements. First stop is Bangkok's largest mall, Siam Paragon (p89); then on to Siam Center and Siam Discovery Center (p88), for books, fashion and design products. But leave most of the day for MBK (p85), which is like an Asian-style market brought indoors. Grab lunch or dinner at one of the mall's food courts, all of which serve up tasty market-style dishes in air-conditioned comfort. After a day of hiding from the elements, enjoy the cooler temperatures of nightfall at the circus of Patpong (Map p95, F2) and the nearby bars and clubs.

## REJUVENATING BANGKOK

There is a peaceful side to this chaotic city – after all most residents pass their time in traffic by meditating. Bangkok's quieter attractions include pretty Dusit Palace Park (p18), where the monarchy built a Thai version of the ornamental Victorian era. Or climb up to the breezy viewpoint from Wat Saket's Golden Mount (p20) and breathe in the fresh air against a skyline of temple spires. Prolong your serenity with a visit to a day spa, such as DVN Spa & Wellbeing Center (p135), which is set in a charming garden enclave, a common feature when Th Sukhumvit was an avenue of the well-to-do. If you're pressed for time, enjoy a straightforward

ITINERARIES

body massage at Ruen-Nuad (p111), which partakes of an equally Thai but more simple setting. A day of relaxation can be rewarded with an evening of gastronomy. Taling Pling (p106) is that rare Bangkok restaurant that stays true to Thai flavours in a stylish setting. Finish off the night amid the old world charm at the Oriental Hotel's Bamboo Bar (p107).

## NIGHTOWL BANGKOK

If your nights are your days, Bangkok is still an entertaining host. In days past, this city was more wild and free-spirited, but the partygoers are a tenacious lot, circumventing city rules with teenage bravado. Bars on and around Th Khao San (p63) rock out every night and continue the party on the streets after closing time. Although Th Khao San is the backpacker ghetto, young Thais are claiming it as a hip scene for indie bands. If you're more of a DJ club butterfly, trek out to Royal City Avenue (p145), an entertainment strip of warehouse-sized clubs. After 2am, cruise over to Th Sukhumvit to Sin Bar (p134) and other after-hours spots. Grab a meal at Soi 38 Night Market (p133) to stave off a hangover. If you're not in bed before daybreak, head to Banglamphu to watch the monks on their morning alms rounds.

### FORWARD PLANNING

It may come as a surprise that Bangkok doesn't require a lot of advance booking. Except for flights and a first-night reservation, you could literally step off the plane and survive swimmingly.

**Three weeks before you go** Watch the web, especially www.asia-hotels.com, for hotel promotions and discounts. Read up on Thai culture and etiquette with the books *Very Thai* by Philip Cornwel-Smith and *Culture Shock! Thailand* by Robert and Nanthapa Cooper. Start following Bangkok news at 2Bangkok.com or the online sites of the English language newspapers, such as *Bangkok Post* (www.bangkokpost.com) and *The Nation* (www.nation multimedia.com).

**One week before you go** Ditch those spaghetti-strap tops for something flouncy and urban but with less decoupage (us Western gals can appear cartoonish in flat-chested Bangkok). Peruse Lonely Planet's Thorntree (thorntree.lonelyplanet.com) for tips on avoiding Bangkok's many scams: dodgy túk-túks or bogus gem and tailor shops.

**The day before you go** Stay out all night so that you'll sleep on the long flight. Hang out in a sauna for weather acclimation. Say bon voyage to your favourite bread and cheese as Bangkok is still on a rice diet. Start dreaming about Thai curries by visiting Real Thai (realthai.blogspot.com).

>NEIGHBOURHOODS

Chitchatting: the unofficial national pastime

# NEIGHBOURHOODS

Bangkok is the 'capital' in every sense of the word. It is Thailand's commercial, creative, economic and consuming centre, attracting rural villagers saddled with debt, globetrotting expats managing multinationals, bilingual high-society types, hip spendthrift teens and small-time import exporters in the city's ethnic enclaves.

Half the fun of 'seeing' Bangkok is getting there – no small task. Bangkok sprawls as impetuously as its most prominent landmark, Mae Nam Chao Phraya (Chao Phraya River). The more predictable railway line heading north from Hualamphong train station neatly divides the central city area into old and new Bangkok.

Old Bangkok cradles Ko Ratanakosin, the original royal district filled with historic monuments. Following the river north is charming Banglamphu, a residential neighbourhood of shophouses and the backpacker spectacle of Th Khao San. Sitting astride Banglamphu like a mahout is Dusit, home to Vimanmek Teak Mansion and the royal residence, Chitlada Palace.

Either side of Hualamphong station is bustling Chinatown; the outer western ring is known as Phahurat (Little India). Further south is the area we define as Riverside, sprinkled with crumbling colonial-style buildings and grand churches.

Newer Bangkok is centered around Silom, Sukhumvit and Siam Square, crammed with skyscrapers, traffic and neon lights. Th Silom is a clogged artery that connects the river to the southern boundary of Lumphini Park and boasts infamous Patpong. Another boundary is Th Withayu and Soi Lang Suan, the work- and play-ground for the diplomatic corps.

Credit-card addicts and fashion-obsessed teenagers leapfrog between shopping centres in the Siam Square area surrounding Th Phra Ram I.

Following Th Phra Ram I east leads to Th Sukhumvit. This is the executive-expat address, where satellite communities of foreigners ease homesickness with visits to restaurants specialising in their respective national dishes.

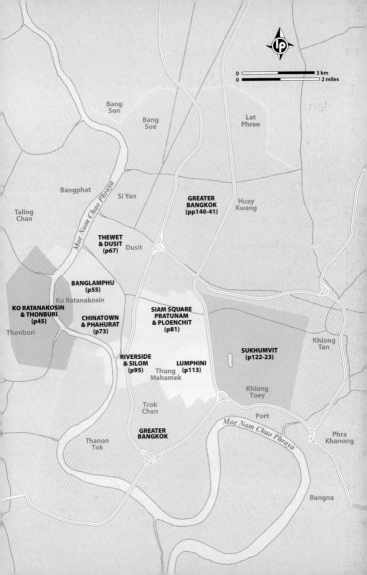

0　　　　　　　3 km
0　　　　　　　2 miles

Bang
Son

Bang
Sue

Lat
Phrao

Bangphat

Si Yan

**GREATER
BANGKOK
(pp140-41)**

Huay
Kwang

Taling
Chan

*Mae Nam Chao Phraya*

**THEWET
& DUSIT
(p67)**

Dusit

**BANGLAMPHU
(p55)**

Ko Ratanakosin

**KO RATANAKOSIN
& THONBURI
(p45)**

**CHINATOWN
& PHAHURAT
(p73)**

Thonburi

**SIAM SQUARE
PRATUNAM
& PLOENCHIT
(p81)**

**SUKHUMVIT
(p122-23)**

Khlong
Tan

**RIVERSIDE
& SILOM
(p95)**

**LUMPHINI
(p113)**

Thung
Mahamek

Khlong
Toey

Trok
Chan

Port

**GREATER
BANGKOK**

*Mae Nam Chao Phraya*

Phra
Khanong

Thanon
Tok

Bangna

# >KO RATANAKOSIN & THONBURI

The first stop for all sightseers, Ko Ratanakosin was the royal centre of Bangkok until the turn of the 20th century. Bounded by both the river and manmade canals, this island district contains important palaces and temples, showcasing Thailand's peculiar marriage of monarchy and religion. More monuments to Thailand's history are found directly across the river in Thonburi, which served briefly as the capital until replaced by Bangkok.

Cultural attractions will dominate your visit here, but the street life will be the ultimate charm. Come early in the morning, before the sun and the crowds reach maximum strength, and stroll the pavements of Th Maharat past the crumbling neoclassical warehouses and small medicine shops. Wander off course along Th Botphram to quieter corners of the old district.

Beware though, rip-off artists prowl this tourist strip. Ignore any stranger who approaches you about an attraction being closed.

## KO RATANAKOSIN & THONBURI

### ◉ SEE
Church of Santa Cruz......1  C6
Grand Palace .................2  C3
Lak Meuang ..................3  C3
Museum of Forensic
Medicine.......................4  A1
National Gallery .............5  C1
National Museum...........6  C1
Royal Barges National
Museum ........................7  A1
Sanam Luang .................8  C2
Silpakorn Art Gallery......9  B3
Wat Arun ....................10  B5

Wat Mahathat .............11  C2
Wat Pho ......................12  C4
Wat Phra Kaew............13  C3
Wat Prayoon................14  D6

### 🛍 SHOP
Amulet Market.............15  B2

### 🍴 EAT
Krisa Coffee Shop.........16  C3
Rub Aroon ...................17  C4
Tha Tien Restaurant.....18  B4

### ⭐ PLAY
National Theatre ..........19  C1
Patravadi Theatre ........20  A2
Wat Mahathat's Dhamma
Talk: Vipassana Meditation
Section ...................... (see 11)
Wat Mahathat's
International Buddhist
Meditation Centre..... (see 11)
Wat Pho Massage
School...........................21  C4

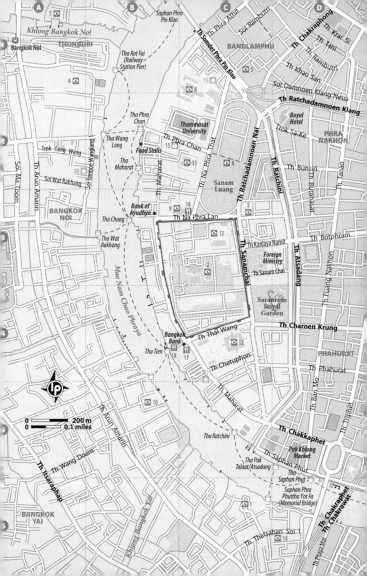

Guardian devils at Wat Arun (p48)

# 👁 SEE

## 📍 GRAND PALACE & WAT PHRA KAEW

☎ 0 2224 1833; www.palaces.thai
.net; Th Na Phra Lan; admission 250B;
🕑 8.30am-3.30pm; 🚌 506, 507, 512,
25, 🚤 Tha Chang; ♿

There is no other site in Thailand
more holy or more famous than
Wat Phra Kaew (Temple of the Emerald Buddha) and the attached
Grand Palace, the former royal
residence. A strict dress code is
enforced: closed-toed shoes, long
pants or skirts, and shirts with
sleeves. You can borrow proper at-
tire from the main office. Remove
your shoes before entering the
main chapel. The admission price
to Grand Palace and Wat Phra
Kaew includes free entrance to
Dusit Palace Park (p18).

## 📍 LAK MEUANG

cnr Th Ratchadamnoen Nai & Th Lak
Meuang; admission free; 🕑 8.30am-
5.30pm; 🚌 506, 507, 🚤 Tha Chang; ♿

A wooden pillar containing the city
guardian (Lak Meuang) is housed
in this shrine, at the southeastern
corner of Sanam Luang. The pillar
was placed here at the found-
ing of the new capital and today
worshippers come and make offerings by commissioning traditional
dances or delivering severed pigs'
heads decorated with incense.

## ☉ MUSEUM OF FORENSIC MEDICINE

☎ 0 2419 7000; 2nd fl, Forensic Pathology Bldg, Siriraj Hospital, Th Phrannok, Thonburi; admission 40B; ☽ 8.30am-4.30pm Mon-Fri; 🚊 Tha Rot Fai

Seriously, do not come to this museum with a full stomach. On display are preserved body parts that have been crushed, shot, stabbed and raped, with grisly before-and-after photos, as well as the entire remains of a notorious Thai murderer.

## ☉ NATIONAL GALLERY

☎ 0 2282 2639; 4 Th Chao Fa; admission 30B; ☽ 9am-4pm Wed-Sun; 🚊 Tha Phra Athit; ♿

Based in the old mint building, this government-funded museum has a very subdued collection of traditional and contemporary art. The general opinion is that this is not the best pedestal for Thailand's artistic traditions, but it is rarely crowded and comfortably air-conditioned. Pieces by Rama VI and Rama IX appeal to royalists.

## ☉ NATIONAL MUSEUM

☎ 0 2224 1402; Th Na Phra That; admission 40B; ☽ 9am-4pm Wed-Sun, free tours 9.30am Wed; 🚌 503, 506, 507, 🚊 Tha Mahathat; ♿

One of the region's best collections of Buddha images resides in this unassuming museum of art

and history. Come for the weekly tours to gain a better appreciation of the undersigned exhibits. For more information, see p27.

## ☉ ROYAL BARGES NATIONAL MUSEUM

☎ 0 2424 0004; Khlong Bangkok Noi, Thonburi; admission 30B (100B to take photos); ☽ 9am-5pm; 🚊 Tha Phra Athit, then tourist shuttle boat

For ceremonial occasions, the elaborately carved barges on display at this modest museum are dusted off for a grand riverine procession. The bows' figureheads depict such Hindu gods as *garuda* (eagle-man and Vishnu's mount), *naga* (multiheaded sea serpent) and *supphannahong* (golden swan). The *Supphannahong* boat traditionally carries the king and is the world's largest dugout.

### PARTING THE WATERS

Dating back to the days of the Ayuthaya court, a royal outing meant a barge procession: hundreds of men rowing sleek, gold-covered boats accompanied by rhythm-makers and royal chanters. In modern times, the elaborate procession is infrequently staged during the *kàthin* ceremony (when robes are offered to monks in a merit-making ritual) or during important anniversaries. The most recent staging of this colourful event was in 2006 to honour the king's 60th year on the throne.

## 🔘 SANAM LUANG

bordered by Th Na Phra That, Th Na Phra Lan, Th Ratchadamnoen Nai, Th Somdet Phra Pin Klao; admission free; ⏰ 5am-8pm; 🚢 Tha Chang; ♿

Lumphini Park may be the green heart of Bangkok but Sanam Luang (Royal Field) is its ceremonial soul. Cremations of members of the royal family and the annual May ploughing ceremony (see p31), which kicks off the rice-growing season, are held here.

## 🔘 SILPAKORN ART GALLERY

☎ 0 2221 1422; 31 Th Na Phra Lan; admission free; ⏰ 9am-7pm Mon-Fri, 10am-5pm Sat; 🚌 503, 506, 508, 12, 44, 🚢 Tha Chang

Corrado Feroci, an Italian artist, is credited for importing modern art to the kingdom. He fell in love with Thailand, adopted a Thai name and founded this fine arts school. The ongoing artistic creations are displayed at the campus gallery, housed in a scenic minor palace.

## 🔘 WAT ARUN

☎ 0 2891 1149; Th Arun Amarin, Thonburi; admission 20B, cross-river ferry 3B; ⏰ 8.30am-5.30pm; 🚢 cross-river ferry from Tha Tien

The precursor to modern skyscrapers, this Khmer-style temple dominates the river landscape like an ancient military installation. Up close, the masculine monument is decorated in delicate mosaic details and marks the re-emergence of the Thai capital after the Burmese invasion in the 18th century. For more information, see p16.

## 🔘 WAT MAHATHAT

☎ 0 2221 5999; 3 Th Maharat; admission 20B; ⏰ 9am-5pm; 🚌 506, 512, 53, 🚢 Tha Maharat or Tha Chang

The centre of learning for the Mahanikai sect of Buddhist monks,

---

### MURAL MASTERS

Thailand's real artistic treasures aren't hung on gallery walls but rather appear as temple murals painted by largely anonymous visual storytellers. Temple murals were used to beautify interiors and explain the story of Buddha and his past lives (Jataka) to a largely illiterate populous. In the corners of these busy painted stages are elements of everyday life – housewives fetching water and fisherman mending nets. Some stunning examples of these visual sermons can be found at **Wat Chong Nonsi** (Map pp140–1; Th Nonsi; ⏰ 8.30am-6pm), which has rare unrenovated Ayuthaya-era murals, and **Wat Suwannaram** (Map pp140–1; Khlong Bangkok Noi; ⏰ 9am-6pm), boasting murals by two pre-eminent artists of the Rama III era. Beginning mural-spotters usually start with **Wat Phra Kaew** (p10) and **Wat Suthat** (p57).

**Virachai Virasuksawadi**
*Head of the Department of Fine Arts' Temple Mural Restoration Team*

**Must-see mural in Bangkok?** The murals at Wat Bowonniwet (p57) are beautiful and are a blend of Thai and Western styles. **Personal favourite temple mural?** The paintings at Wat Suwannaram (opposite) in Thonburi show amazing skill. **Examples of quirky or unusual Thai murals in Bangkok?** The murals along the inside walls of the compound at Wat Phra Kaew (p46) are known for their depiction of the *Ramakian*, but they also include scenes from every day Thai life, including smoking ganja. **How are temple murals in Bangkok different than elsewhere?** Most temple murals in Bangkok were painted by high-ranking artists and depict elite life. If you go to temples outside Bangkok you'll find much more 'folk art' showing the every day life of common people.

*By Austin Bush*

Wat Mahathat is a workaday temple lacking in red carpet appeal. Instead come to take part in the ordinary life of a Thai temple: making merit or studying meditation (p53). For more information on Wat Mahathat, see p22.

### ☺ WAT PHO

☎ 2221 9911; Th Chetuphon & Th Sanamchai; admission 50B; ☽ 8am-6pm; 🚌 506, 507, 25, ⚓ Tha Tien or Tha Chang; ♿

Second on the tourists' itinerary after Wat Phra Kaew, this temple has many more curious corners (and traditional massage pavilions) to explore beyond the crowd-pleasing reclining Buddha, a 46m long and 15m high figure illustrating Buddha's passing into nirvana. It is also home to the largest collection of Buddha images in the country and the earliest centre for public eduction. For more information on the temple complex, see p14.

### ☺ WAT PRAYOON

cnr 24 Th Prachadhipok & Th Thetsaban Sai 1; donations accepted; ☽ 8am-6pm; ⚓ cross-river ferry from Tha Pak Talaad (Atsadang); ♿

Near the old Portuguese quarter in Thonburi, beside Memorial Bridge and the banks of Mae Nam Chao Phraya, is this unusual temple complex. Within the grounds, an artificial hill, built under the orders of Rama III, is littered with curious miniature shrines, and little temples. Nearby, fruit vendors sell snacks for children to feed to the resident turtles.

## 🛍 SHOP

### ☐ AMULET MARKET _Market_

Th Maharat; ☽ 9am-5pm; 🚌 506, 512, 53, ⚓ Tha Maharat or Tha Chang

If you need a charm to stop bullets or even a set of pre-owned dentures, wander through this streetside market catering to fate and fortune and the ability to

### WORTH THE TRIP

When Bangkok was a port of call, Western nations sailed in to stake a claim in the lucrative Asia sea trade. Centred around the Oriental Hotel were the headquarters of shipping interests, the French embassy and Christian churches. The biggest church-builders were the Portuguese, one of the first Europeans in the kingdom (due in part to their nearby colony of Malacca in Malaysia). They were given prime riverside real estate in recognition for their contribution in securing the new capital after the fall of Ayuthaya. The surviving churches, **Holy Rosary Church** (Map p95; Th Yotha) and **Church of Santa Cruz** (Soi Kuti Jiin, Thonburi), are still in operation and boast parishes of many former Indochinese citizens.

Get your custom-made protection at the Amulet Market

alter the two. The amulet market begins on the sidewalks of Th Maharat and follows the narrow *soi* (lanes) that lead to the river. For more information, see p22.

# 🍴 EAT

## 🍴 KRISA COFFEE SHOP *Thai* $
☎ 0 2225 2680; Th Na Phra Lan; 🕑 10am-6pm; 🚌 506, 512, 🚢 Tha Chang; ♿
Beat the heat during a temple tour with a pit stop at this cosy café. It's air-conditioned and serves

up cheap and cheerful one-plate meals, such as *kŭaytĭaw phàt khîi mao* (wide rice noodles with holy basil and chilli), to see you through the expedition.

## 🍴 RUB AROON *Thai* $$
Th Maharat; 🕑 10am-7pm; 🚢 Tha Tien; ♿ ♨ Ⓥ
This traveller-friendly café is a pleasant escape from sightseeing in Ko Ratanakosin. The restored shopfront opens directly out to the street with cosy seating and patient service. The dishes are

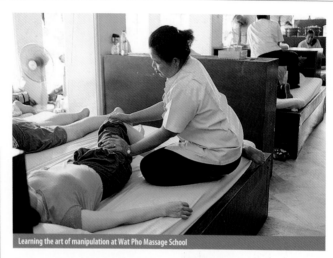
Learning the art of manipulation at Wat Pho Massage School

basic and delicious, served alongside fruit drinks and coffees for sipping away tropical fatigue.

## 🍴 THA TIEN RESTAURANT
*Thai* $$

**Tha Tien, Th Maharat;** ⏱ **7.30-midnight;** 🚌 **512;** 🚶

After the river express boat ends its evening service, this pier-side restaurant fires up the wok and takes in a spotlighted view of Wat Arun. Cheap, yummy and very rustic, Tha Tien's added bonus is that it offers a chance to soak in the local ways: whiskey as a main course and boat vendors selling dried cuttlefish.

## ⭐ PLAY

### ⭐ NATIONAL THEATRE *Theatre*
☎ **0 2224 1342; 2 Th Ratchini; 50-200B;** 🚌 **511, 53,** 🚢 **Tha Mahathat;** 🚶

The National Theatre has kept *khon* dance-drama alive through its slumps in popularity. But presently the theatre is in a bit of a slump. It still hosts traditional Thai dance performances but the schedule is erratic; ask at the theatre or at the Bangkok Tourist Division (p205).

### ⭐ PATRAVADI THEATRE *Theatre*
☎ **0 2412 7287; www.patravaditheatre .com; cnr Soi Wat Rakhang & Soi Tambon Wanglang 1, Thonburi; 300-800B;**

⊙ schedule varies; 👤 private cross-river ferry from Tha Maharat; ♿ Patravadi is Bangkok's only open-air theatre and one of its most avant-garde. Led by Patravadi Mejudhon, a famous Thai actor and playwright, the troupe's performances blend traditional Thai dance with modern choreography, music and costume.

### ⭐ WAT MAHATHAT'S DHAMMA TALK: VIPASSANA MEDITATION SECTION
*Meditation*

☎ 0 2623 5881; www.mcu.ac.th/IBMC; Room 105, Maha Chula Bldg, Maha Chulalongkorn Rajavidyalaya University, Wat Mahathat; admission free; ⊙ 3-5pm every 2nd & 4th Sat; 🚌 506, 53, 👤 Tha Chang

Twice a month, lectures in English on Buddhism are held at Maha Chulalongkorn Rajavidyalaya University, Southeast Asia's most important place of Buddhist study.

**A MINDFUL VISIT**

Short-term meditation instruction is available to foreign visitors at temples like Wat Mahathat (p22) as well as retreat centres such as House of Dhamma (p145). Respect for the teacher is of paramount importance, and many long-term sessions include opening and closing ceremonies honouring their teachers.

### ⭐ WAT MAHATHAT'S INTERNATIONAL BUDDHIST MEDITATION CENTRE
*Meditation*

☎ 0 2222 6011; www.mcu.ac.th/IBMC; Section 5, Wat Mahathat 3, Th Maharat; donations accepted; ⊙ 7am, 1pm & 6pm; 🚌 506, 53, 👤 Tha Chang

The International Buddhist Meditation Centre (IBMC) at Wat Mahathat is where most Westerners study *satipatthana* (mindful meditation) in Bangkok. Classes are held three times daily and participants are welcome to join the meditation periods or adhere to a more strict immersion into temple life with residential courses.

### ⭐ WAT PHO MASSAGE SCHOOL *Massage*

☎ 0 2221 3686; Soi Penphat, Th Maharat; ⊙ 8am-5pm; 🚌 507, 👤 Tha Tien; ♿

The primary training school for Thai massage also has an air-conditioned drop-in centre for exhausted sightseers needing a little kneading. If impressed by their work, you might consider enrolling in one of the multi-week classes on different aspects of this traditional art. There are also massage salons with fans on the temple grounds. Keep in mind that Soi Penphat is not signed.

# >BANGLAMPHU

Easily Bangkok's most charming neighbourhood, Banglamphu is the city's former aristocratic enclave, once filled with minor royalty and riverside manses. Today the old quarter is dominated by backpackers seeking R&R on famous Th Khao San, civil servants sauntering between offices and lunch spots and Bangkok's only enclave of bohemian artists and students. In Banglamphu, trees still outnumber high-rises and monks make their morning alms route often before the backpackers have consumed last call. The travellers amenities are thick and cheap in this neighbourhood: you'll find loads of souvenir shopping and late-night imbibing. On the edges of the tourist zone there are a maze of two-storey shophouses, each decorated with terracotta water gardens or potted plants and low-hanging shades that block out the mean sun. Vendor carts are plentiful in this area, so is people-watching and unfettered wandering. To catch a better glimpse into daily Thai life, wander the *soi* that branch off Th Samsen, on the northern side of Khlong Banglamphu or check out the nationalistic paraphernalia shops on Th Phra Sumen.

## BANGLAMPHU

## SEE

The gateway to Banglamphu is along Th Ratchadamnoen Klang, a wide European-style boulevard lined with billboard-sized pictures of the king and the royal family. The showcase attractions along the royal boulevard are picturesquely lit at night giving the illusion of a picture-book fantasy of the exotic East.

### DEMOCRACY MONUMENT

**cnr Th Ratchadamnoen Klang & Th Din So; admission free;** 511, 512, 44, **Tha Phra Athit**

Four-pronged Democracy Monument holds a key place in Bangkok's political history. Built to commemorate the nation's transition from absolute monarchy to constitutional monarchy in 1932, the monument is the

natural home of pro-democracy rallies, including the tragic demonstrations of 1992 that turned bloody at the hands of the military.

### QUEEN'S GALLERY

☎ 0 2281 5360; www.queengallery.org; **101 Th Ratchadamnoen Klang; admission 20B;** 10am-7pm Thu-Tue; 511, 512, 2, **khlong taxi to Tha Phan Fah**

A project funded by the queen, this museum presents paintings and sculpture by renowned domestic and international artists. Most Thai artists featured at the Queen's Gallery have been recognised as National Artists or receive funding through the queen's SUPPORT foundation for the preservation of handicrafts.

### SANTICHAIPRAKAN PARK & PHRA SUMEN FORT

**cnr Th Phra Athit; admission free;** 5am-8pm; 506, 53, **Tha Phra Athit;**

It's a tiny patch of greenery with a great river view and lots of evening action, including comical communal aerobics classes. The riverside pathway heading southwards makes for a serene promenade. The park's most prominent landmark is the blindingly white Phra Sumen Fort, which was built in 1783 to defend the city against a river invasion.

**AREAS OF INTEREST**

The district of Phra Nakhon slumbers beside touristy Ko Ratanakosin with a handful of neoclassical buildings and antique businesses. On Th Boriphat, just a block from Wat Saket are several wood shops that sell teak components for the upkeep of traditional Thai houses.

A block from the Giant Swing and Wat Suthat on Th Botphram is a collection of religious paraphernalia shops that sell Buddha figures and devotional items purchased by wealthy merit-makers.

## BELOVED CROWN & COUNTRY

The king, nation and religion are indescribably linked in Thailand, but a walk along Th Phra Sumen can help illustrate it. Start at Wat Bowonniwet which is the 'royal' temple: it and the affiliated Thammayut reformation sect was founded by Rama IV (King Mongkut), who served as the temple's first abbot. Rama IV was a scholar before a monarch and wished to expunge some of the superstitious elements out of Thai Buddhism. Successive kings have been ordained here and the sect continues a close relationship with the crown. The temple itself betrays little of this connection but the nearby shophouses heading east toward Th Prachathipathai sell full-size pictures of the king, national and religious flags and other paraphernalia of the Thai triumvirate.

### ◎ WAT BOWONNIWET

cnr Th Phra Sumen & Th Tanao; donations accepted; ⏱ 8am-5.30pm; 🚌 15, 53, ⛴ Tha Phra Athit; ♿

Home to the Buddhist Maha-makut University, this royally affiliated monastery is the national headquarters of the Thammayut sect of Thai Buddhism. It may be in ultra-casual Banglamphu but it's also where the present king was ordained. Visitors must dress appropriately.

### ◎ WAT RATCHANATDA

☎ 0 2224 8807; cnr Th Ratchadam-noen Klang & Th Mahachai; donations accepted; ⏱ 9am-5pm; 🚌 503, 59, ⛴ khlong taxi to Tha Phan Fah; ♿

Across Th Mahachai from Wat Saket, Wat Ratchanatda was built for Rama III's granddaughter. Today this temple is better known for its metallic castlelike monastery, with many passageways and meditation cells at each intersection.

### ◎ WAT SAKET & GOLDEN MOUNT

☎ 0 2621 0576; Th Chakkaphatdi; admission 10B; ⏱ 7.30am-5.30pm; 🚌 508, 511, ⛴ khlong taxi to Tha Phan Fah

A less conspicuous member of the temple itinerary, Wat Saket boasts an artificial hill from which Bangkok appears meditatively serene. Join the candlelit procession to the summit in November during the temple fair. See also p20.

### ◎ WAT SUTHAT & GIANT SWING

☎ 0 2224 9845; Th Bamrung Meuang; admission 20B; ⏱ 9am-8pm; 🚌 508, ⛴ khlong taxi to Tha Phan Fah

Wat Suthat holds the highest royal temple grade. Inside the *wíhǎan* (sanctuary for a Buddha sculpture) are intricate *Jataka* murals and Thailand's biggest surviving Sukhothai-era bronze Buddha. Over the road is the Giant Swing (Sao Ching-Cha), site of a former Brahman festival in honour of Shiva.

#  SHOP

You'll be magnetically drawn to Banglamphu for shopping. Vendors line all of Th Khao San from mid-morning to late night selling every possible souvenir and even an evolving selection of funky fashion. This is a bargaining district so don't forget to haggle, which is considered normal procedure if done with a smile and a spirit of goodwill.

## 📷 KHAO SAN MARKET *Market*
**Th Khao San;** 🕑 **10am-11pm Tue-Sun;** 🚌 **503, 511, 53,** 🚢 **Tha Phra Athit;** ♿
Got a grubby backpack that needs filling? Stocking up on the gifts and souvenirs that line the Southeast Asia pancake trail: hair-braids, bootleg CDs, Thai knick-knacks and hippy jewellery. At night the selection targets the fashion-conscious Thai teens. The sizes fit us burly folks, the prices are penny-pinching cheap and there's always someone misbehaving.

## 📷 MONK'S BOWL VILLAGE *Handicrafts*
**Soi Baan Baht, Th Bamrung Meuang;** 🕑 **10am-8pm;** 🚌 **508,** 🚢 **khlong taxi to Tha Pan Fah;** ♿
The only surviving village of three founded by Rama I, Baan Baht (Monk's Bowl Village) still hand-hammers eight pieces of steel (representing Buddha's eightfold path) into the distinctive alms bowls used by monks to receive morning food donations. Tourists instead of temples are the primary patrons these days and a bowl purchase is usually rewarded with a demonstration.

## 📷 NITTAYA CURRY SHOP *Cooking Supplies*
☎ **0 2282 8212; 136-40 Th Chakraphong;** 🕑 **10am-7pm;** 🚌 **506, 17,** 🚢 **Tha Phra Athit**
Fresh markets are filled with conical-shaped mountains of curry paste that simplify the dinner routine for many home cooks.

## DRIVING A HARD BARGAIN
Thais respect a good bargainer, someone who can get a reasonable price without either seller or buyer losing face. Here are some hints:
> Do your homework on prices
> Don't start bargaining unless you intend to buy
> Always let the vendor make the first offer and then ask 'can you discount the price?'
> Don't be aggressive or raise your voice; be friendly
> Remember that there's a fine line between bargaining and niggling; it is considered poor form to argue over 10B

Lost baggage? Buy an entire wardrobe at the markets on Th Khao San

If you'd like your own reserve of high-quality paste, stop into this neighbourhood curry shop, which sells vacuum-sealed bags of green, red and yellow curry ready to use for post-trip dinner parties. Also check out the snack and gift sections.

### 📷 PASSPORT BOOKSHOP Books
☎ 0 2629 0694; 523 Th Phra Sumen; 🕑 noon-6pm; 🚤 Tha Phra Athit; 🦽 fair
This quirky little shop is a good friend to have. The affable owners are Banglamphu bohemians and love to talk books. The store carries unusual art books and graphic novels, many from small independent publishers.

### 📷 RIM KHOB FAH BOOKSTORE Books
☎ 0 2622 3510; 78/1 Th Ratchadamnoen; 🕑 8.30am-7pm; 🚌 511, 512, 🚤 Tha Phan Fah; 🦽
For the pseudo nerds, this bookstore has lots of glossy books on Thai arts and culture. Without committing loads of baht, you can sample an array of skinny scholarly publications from the Fine Arts Department on such topics as *What is a Buddha Image?*

### 📷 TAKEE TAAKON Handicrafts
☎ 0 2629 1473; 118 Th Phra Athit; 🕑 10am-5pm Mon-Sat; 🚌 53, 🚤 Tha Phra Athit
This shop has a beautiful selection of handwoven textiles from silk-producing regions, especially

A barbecue vendor prepares grilled delicacies before the crowds descend

northern Thailand. If mum won't dig another wooden elephant, you'll also find a small assortment of classy handicraft souvenirs.

# 🍴 EAT

Banglamphu is a great neighbourhood to graze in. Vendor carts make a patchwork quilt of the district, allowing ample sightseeing for a roving stomach. Thanks to the backpackers, vegetarians will find more sympathetic options here than elsewhere in this meat-loving city. The restaurants are casual and often spare on ambience, leaving more flair for the food.

🍴 **ARAWY** *Thai Vegetarian* $
**152 Th Din So;** 🕑 **7am-7pm;** 🚌 **511, 35,** 🚤 **khlong taxi to Tha Phan Fah;** ♿ ♨ **V**
Curry-in-a-hurry is the aim of this tiny and inconspicuous veggie spot marked by a roman-script sign reading 'Alloy'. Arawy was one of the city's first vegetarian restaurants and it's still going strong, serving pre-made dishes such as pumpkin stir-fry and green curry.

🍴 **CHOSHANA** *Israeli*  $

**sub-soi off Th Chakraphong** 🕙 **11am-11pm** 🚌 **503, 511,** 🚢 **Tha Phra Athit;** ♿ 🚼 V

Down an alley beside the petrol station on Th Chakraphong, Choshana's is a favourite of cuisine-cruising travellers. The falafel-and-hummus plates are suitable gut bombs, but don't overlook the tasty *baba ghanoush*.

🍴 **CHOTE CHITR** *Thai*  $

☎ **0 2221 4082; 146 Th Phraeng Phuton;** 🕙 **10am-10pm Mon-Sat;** 🚌 **508, 48;** 🚼

Antique family-owned restaurants adorn this old section of town where middle-class Thais eat the way their parents and grandparents did before them. Chote Chitr is famous for *mee krob*, sweet-and-spicy crispy fried noodles,

and the banana flower salad *(yum hua plee)*. *New York Times* food reviewer RW Apple ate here and loved it. It's located off Th Tanao.

🍴 **HEMLOCK** *Thai*  $$

☎ **0 2282 7507; 56 Th Phra Athit;** 🕙 **5.30-11.30pm;** 🚌 **53,** 🚢 **khlong taxi to Tha Phra Athit;** ♿ V

You've met this restaurant before – remember that cosy gem where you wooed countless dates? Hemlock is just such a creature, boasting a steady cast of artsy types and a menu that reads like old literature.

🍴 **ISAN RESTAURANTS** *Northeastern Thai*  $$

**Th Ratchadamnoen Nok;** 🕙 **11am-10pm;** 🚌 **503, 509, 70;** ♿ 🚼

When a boxing match is on at nearby Ratchadamnoen Stadium, these restaurants are run off their feet serving plates of Isan staples like *kài yâang* (grilled chicken), *sôm-tam* (green papaya salad) and *khâo nǐaw* (sticky rice). A fun pre-match tradition, but the chicken is too dry to qualify as a main event.

🍴 **KHRUA NOPPARAT** *Thai*  $

☎ **0 2281 7578; 136 Th Phra Athit;** 🕙 **10.30am-9.30pm Mon-Sat;** 🚌 **53,** 🚢 **Tha Phra Athit;** ♿ 🚼 V

It may have a groovy factor of zilch but the food factor rockets off the

NEIGHBOURHOODS

BANGLAMPHU

## BALANCING ACT

Thai cuisine's primary ingredient is balance. To understand this, just look at a typical Thai table, usually decorated with a condiment caddy containing the four key flavours – chilli to adjust the heat, fish sauce for saltiness, vinegar with chilli for sourness and sugar for sweetness. A little bit of this, more of that and voilà you've become a truly Thai eater.

scale. Thai families and workmates crowd this joint to eat plates of yummy everyday Thai dishes at little more than street prices.

### 🍴 RICKY'S COFFEE SHOP
*International*                                  $$

☎ 0 2846 3011; 22 Th Phra Athit;
🕑 8am-10pm; 🚌 53, 🛥 Tha Phra Athit; ⓖ Ⓥ

Ricky's is a beautiful café, decorated like an old Chinese tea shop and decked out with old fans and cigarette poster-girl prints. And it knows its road-warrior market well, serving the best filled baguettes in Banglamphu. Pity about the unreliable service and bland Thai food.

### 🍴 ROTI-MATABA
*Southern Thai-Muslim*                          $

☎ 0 2282 2119; 136 Th Phra Athit;
🕑 7am-8pm Tue-Sun; 🚌 53, 🛥 Tha Phra Athit; ⓖ

Don't visit Banglamphu without stopping by Roti-Mataba. The rhythms of the roti makers as they slap and flip the Indian-style flatbread on the hotplate will draw you in. But spooning chicken korma or southern Thai-style curries onto bites of crunchy roti will make your tastebuds respect you.

### 🍴 THIP SAMAI *Thai*                        $

☎ 0 2221 6280; 313 Th Mahachai;
🕑 5.30pm-2am; 🚌 511, 35, 🛥 khlong taxi to Tha Phan Fah; ⓖ ⓖ

The country's most common street food, *phàt thai*, still retains its venerable footpath setting but it has been elevated (flavourwise) to notoriety here at Thip Samai. Wrapped in a delicate egg crepe, the special noodles are spiked with prime shrimp and achieve the perfect texture. It must be seriously good if Thais are willing to pay this much (60B) for a plate of noodles.

## CALLING ALL DAREDEVILS

Silly you – the average garden pest is really a tasty treat. After the wet season, vendors appear throughout town (try Th Khao San) with conical heaps of stir-fried bugs (crickets, red ants and water beetles). Pull off the legs and pop the bugger in your mouth, after which initial revulsion will turn into potato-chip-like addiction.

In the mood for love at a streetside neighbourhood restaurant

### 🍴 TOM YUM KUNG *Thai* $$
☎ 0 2629 1818; Th Khao San; ⏱ noon-1.30am; 🚌 503, 511; ⚙ ♨

We don't make a habit of recommending restaurants on Th Khao San; it is just too easy to get caught in a tourist trap. But Tom Yum Kung is better known among Thais than foreigners and the dishes prove it. No silly pineapple curries here.

### 🍴 TON PHO *Thai* $$
☎ 0 2280 0452; Th Phra Athit; ⏱ 11am-10pm; 🚌 53, ⛴ Tha Phra Athit; ⚙ ♨ Ⓥ

On a steamy day, try to catch a breeze at this open-air riverside restaurant, just beside Tha Phra Athit. Ceiling fans rotate relentlessly overhead, as waiters scurry across the wooden floorboards (big gaps reveal the river beneath) with excellent Thai-style salads and seafood.

## 🍸 DRINK

Th Khao San is hands down one of the must-see watering holes in the city. After sundown, the street becomes an open saloon brimming with VW vans selling hummingbird

Even Th Khao San offers moments of respite

syrup cocktails and sidewalk tables littered with beer bottles. There's also a de facto human parade: exuberant backpackers, rebellious Thai youths and even a few curious yuppie Thais. The party snakes through to Th Rambutri and Soi Rambutri, on either side of Th Chakraphong.

### ▼ AD HERE THE 13TH *Bar*
13 Th Samsen; ⏲ music 10pm-midnight; 🚌 30, 🛥 Tha Phra Athit
The best little dive bar in Thailand, Ad Here the 13th is a homey

meeting place in which to have too many late nights and countless suds and cigs. The house band steered by guitarist Pong and vocalist Georgia melt the night and the regulars' hearts with smoking blues tunes and rocking classics.

### ▼ ILLY CAFÉ *Bar*
☎ 0 2281 4445; 95 Th Chakraphong; 🚌 53, 🛥 Tha Phra Athit
Eclectic and funky, Illy Café is a restaurant by day and a 30-something bar at night. The vintage décor captures Banglamphu's bohemian aesthetic and egalitarian spirit.

### ▼ PHRANAKORN BAR *Bar*
☎ 0 2282 7507; 58/2 Soi Damnoen Klang Tai; ⏲ 6pm-midnight; 🚌 511 & 512, 🛥 Tha Phra Athit
A well-kept secret that Lonely Planet has finally sniffed out, Phranakorn Bar is just steps away from Th Khao San but worlds removed. Students and arty types make this a home away from hovel with modest gallery exhibits, but the real draw at Phranakorn Bar is a rooftop terrace for beholding the old district's majesty.

### ▼ TO-SIT *Bar*
☎ 0 2629 1199; 24 Th Phra Athit; 🚌 53, 🛥 Tha Phra Athit
A closet-sized bar on arty Th Phra Athit, To-Sit attracts a student

## KHLONG FERRY: THE LOCALS' SHORTCUT

Forget about trying to get in or out of Banglamphu during rush hour. Even the miliary has to contend with the district's clogged arteries: they staged the 2006 coup around midnight, the best time to avoid gridlock. But the locals know that the area's one remaining canal, famously polluted Khlong Saen Saeb, is a friend indeed during commute time. Even if you're not an office worker, the crafty boats that ply the canal provide a quintessential flight through the City of Angels. (Just remember to cover your face if the boat hits any wake to avoid contact with septic water and hold on tight when climbing on or off the boat.) You can catch the *khlong* ferry from Tha Phan Fah, near Wat Saket, to reach the Siam Square area (Tha Ratchathewi); boats run from 6am to 7pm and cost from 8B to 20B, depending on the stop.

crowd who come in for the rounds of Thai whiskey and lost-love anthems sung by a solo guitarist.

# ⭐ PLAY

⭐ ANGELA BEAUTY CARE *Spa*
☎ 0 2282 7921; 329 Th Rambutri; 1½ hr facial 500B; ⏲ 8am-10.30pm; 🚢 Tha Phra Athit ♿

The super nanny of facials, Angela Beauty Care will restore order to clogged pores. There is no luxury or pampering at this salon, just a whole lot of straightforward, unadulterated zit popping, exfoliating and masking to erase signs of puberty.

⭐ RATCHADAMNOEN BOXING STADIUM *Muay Thai*
☎ 0 2281 4205; Th Ratchadamnoen Nok; 🚌 503, 509

*Muay thai* fights are held at this bare bones stadium four times a week: Monday, Wednesday and Thursday at 6pm, and Sunday at 5pm. Tickets cost 1000/1500/2000B (3rd class/2nd class/ringside). The stadium doesn't usually fill up until the main event around 8pm. As a prematch warm-up, catch a plate of *kài yâang* (grilled chicken) and other northeastern dishes from the restaurants surrounding the stadium.

# >THEWET & DUSIT

Rama V (King Chulalongkorn; r 1868–1910) returned from his grand tour of Europe with a building itch. He wanted his kingdom to reflect the regal flair he had witnessed in Europe. And so a new royal district was constructed in the area of Dusit, which was once a fruit orchard.

As a result, the roads in Dusit are boulevards instead of converted canals and Rama V's new palace is fanciful and Victorian. But the unprecedented planning that went into creating Dusit left it uncharacteristically sterile for cramped and hyperactive Bangkok. The monuments to modern Thailand may look lovely from a car window however the broad foot-paths are empty of street life, drawing more attention to the tropical heat than smart urban planning. After visiting Dusit Palace, the former royal residence, hop in a cab or túk-túk over to the riverside section of the district, referred to as Thewet, for an elixir of Bangkok village life, complete with markets, kids playing badminton and novice monks feeding the fish at the Thewet ferry pier.

## THEWET & DUSIT

Th Sukhothai

Th Pichai

Khlong Khem Prechakon

Th Phra Ram V

Chitlada
Park

Royal Turf
Club

N

200 m
0.1 miles

Th Ratchawithi

Th Suphan

Dusit Zoo

Th U-thong Nai

Th Nakhon Pathom

HM King
Bhumibol
Photography
Exhibitions

Dusit
Palace
Park

Th Sri Ayuthaya

Royal
Plaza

Th Likhit

Th Ratchadamnoen Nok

Th Ratchasima

DUSIT

Amphon
Park

Soi 12

Th Phitsanulok

Th Luk Luang

Th Krung Kasem

Khlong Phadung Krung Kasem

Th Prachathipat

Sol 13
Sol 11

Soi Chaiyot

Sol 9

Church of the
Immaculate
Conception

National
Library

Th Sri Ayuthaya

THEWET

Soi Thewet 1

BANGKAMPHU

#  SEE

## ◎ ABHISEK DUSIT THRONE HALL

☎ 0 2628 6300; Dusit Palace Park, Th Ratchawithi; ticket for all Dusit Palace Park sights 250B, free with Grand Palace ticket; ⏱ 9.30am-4pm; 🚌 510, 72; ♿
This Moorish-inspired building displays traditional Thai handicrafts, such as silverware, blocks of teak carved into florid detail and geometrically patterned bamboo baskets. The pieces are made by members of the Foundation for the Promotion of Supplementary Occupations and Related Techniques (Support), which has been set up to keep traditional skills alive and is sponsored by Queen Sirikit.

## ◎ ANCIENT CLOTH MUSEUM

☎ 0 2628 6300; Dusit Palace Park, Th Ratchawithi; ticket for all Dusit Palace Park sights 250B, free with Grand Palace ticket; ⏱ 9.30am-4pm; 🚌 510, 72; ♿
If you're interested in fashion, you should enjoy a poke around this museum, with its well-annotated collection of royal cloth and royals wearing cloth (Queen Sirikit looks a bit groovy in the old B&W photos).

## ◎ CHITLADA PALACE

cnr Th Ratchawithi & Th Phra Ram V, Dusit; ⏱ closed to the public; 🚌 510, 512
The current royal family's residence, Chitlada Palace is also a royally funded agriculture

Moorish design and Thai handicrafts at Abhisek Dusit Throne Hall

centre demonstrating the reigning king's commitment to the progress of the country's major industry. The palace is not open to the public and it's pretty difficult to see from the outside, but you can spot rice paddies and animal pastures – smack in the middle of Bangkok – through the perimeter fence.

### ⓒ DUSIT PALACE PARK
☎ 0 2628 6300; bounded by Th Ratchawithi, Th U-Thong & Th Ratchasima; ticket for all Dusit Palace Park sights 250B, free with Grand Palace ticket; ⌚ 9.30am-4pm; 🚌 510, 72; ♿
Oh-so-dainty Dusit Palace is the Thai monarchy's nod to the Victorian era. It contains Vimanmek Palace, the world's largest teak mansion, pleasant manicured grounds and the Ancient Cloth Museum and Royal Thai Elephant Museum, plus daily traditional dance performances (10.30am and 2pm). For more information, see p18.

### ⓒ DUSIT ZOO
☎ 0 2281 2000; Th Phra Ram V; 100/50B; ⌚ 8am-9pm; 🚌 510, 18, ⛴ Tha Thewet; ♿
It would be easy to spend a day here. The peaceful grounds of this zoo, which once hosted the royal botanical garden, have a plethora of eateries as well as a

Fish-feeding frenzy, Tha Thewet

playground and a big lake for paddle-boating. The animal-housing areas are not the most modern or inviting. Located between Th Ratchawithi and Th Sri Ayuthaya.

### ⓒ ROYAL THAI ELEPHANT MUSEUM
☎ 0 2628 6300; Dusit Palace Park, Th Ratchawithi; ticket for all Dusit Palace Park sights 250B, free with Grand Palace ticket; ⌚ 9.30am-4pm; 🚌 510, 72; ♿
Thais consider albinism auspicious, so all white elephants are considered royal property (Rama

Learn all about the history of these unforgettable creatures at the Royal Thai Elephant Museum (p69)

IX keeps one at his palace). Dusit Palace had two stables for keeping white elephants and this museum remembers these lucky creatures with displays explaining the ranks of elephants and their important role in Thai society.

### THEWET FLOWER MARKET
*Market*

**Th Krung Kasem;** 🕐 **10am-6pm;** 🛥 **Tha Thewet**

Hardly a practical shopping option, this open-air market, located off Th Samsen, is more for windowless window shopping than actual purchases. You'll discover from the selection that Bangkokians are avid container gardeners

and can grow orchids and other exotic plants with minimal care.

### VIMANMEK PALACE
☎ **0 2628 6300; Dusit Palace Park, Th Ratchawithi; ticket for all Dusit Palace Park sights 250B, free with Grand Palace ticket;** 🕐 **9.30am-4pm;** 🚌 **510, 72;** ♿

This teak mansion was originally located on an island in the Gulf of Thailand, but was dismantled and reassembled, reputedly without nails, in 1901. Rama V took a three-storey octagonal apartment for himself and decorated his new home like the grand Victorian palaces he had seen in Europe. Women lived in a special green-coloured wing (the only men

**RAINY DAY TAXI**
It never fails: when you need to get across town, the skies will unleash a monsoon storm. Bangkok's already crippled road transport starts to drown and cab drivers hold the coveted life-savers. Taxi drivers make their money with the flag fall not with distance and definitely not from sitting in traffic. When the rains bring an increase of customers, the cabbies become picky, taking people who need a quick ride and turning down people who need more of a commitment. Don't take a stern headshake personally, it's only business in Bangkok.

allowed inside were Rama V, a monk, a doctor and small boys). Viewing of the mansion is by guided tour only; tours run every 30 minutes.

### ◉ WAT BENCHAMABOPHIT
cnr Th Sri Ayuthaya & Th Phra Ram V; 20B; ☺ 8am-5.30pm; 🚍 513; ♿
Buddha image buffs find Wat Benchamabophit fascinating. Known

as the 'Marble Temple' (it's made of white Carrara marble), it has a collection of 53 Buddha images representing different figures and styles from Thailand and other Buddhist countries. It was built during Rama V's reign, the temple's central Buddha image contains his ashes, and its cruciform *bòt* (central chapel) is a pure example of contemporary wat architecture.

## 🛍 SHOP
### 🛍 CHITLADA SHOP
*Handicrafts*
☎ 0 2282 8435; Chitlada Palace, Th Ratchawithi; ☺ 10am-4.30pm; 🚍 510, 18, 28; ♿
This is probably as close as you'll get to the royal family, so remember to dress respectfully (women must wear long skirts and closed shoes to gain entrance). Located at the palace, this is an outlet of the nonprofit Support organisation which promotes traditional craft-making skills.

# >CHINATOWN & PHAHURAT

Bangkok owes much of its urban identity to the labourers who left the Teochew region of China in the late 1700s in the hopes of finding their fortune in Siam. Many built mercantile empires in this riverside area from a few scraps of entrepreneurial brawn. Although many of the descendants have graduated into the elite strata of Bangkok society, Chinatown still retains its distinctive tie to the homeland with undiluted commerce. Shark-fin restaurants, gold and jade shops and huge neon signs in Chinese characters line Th Yaowarat, the district's main street. In the shadowy alleys, goods are unloaded by hand from crumbling warehouses and machine repair shops stain the footpaths with motor oil.

To see Chinatown in business, come during the daylight to explore the various markets. But to savour Chinatown, come in the evenings when the streets off Th Yaowarat become nightly food markets.

Around the intersection of Th Phahurat and Th Chakraphet is a small but thriving Indian district, generally called Phahurat or Little India. Cramped storefronts are dominated by gem traders and fabric merchants.

For more information on this area, see p15.

## CHINATOWN & PHAHURAT

**WORTH THE TRIP**

Chinatown is organised like an ancient guild system – merchants of a feather flock together. Here's a guide to the streets and their mercantile persuasions.

> Th Charoen Krung: Chinatown's primary thoroughfare begins at the intersection of Th Mahachai with a collection of old record stores. Nearby Talat Khlong Ong Ang sells used, disused, and unused electronic gadgets. Nakhon Kasem is the reformed thieves market now stocking gadgets for portable food prep. Further east, Talat Khlong Thom is a hardware centre. West of Th Ratchawong, the stores cater to the after life and the passing of life.

> Th Yaowarat: this is Bangkok's gold street, the biggest trading centre of the precious metal in the country. Near the intersection of Th Ratchawong, stores shift to souvenirs for Chinese and Singaporean tourists. Tucked between the knick-knacks are a few apothecaries that smell like wood bark and ancient secrets.

> Th Mittraphan: signmakers branch off Wong Wian 22 Karakada; Thai and roman letters are typically cut out by a hand-guided lathe placed prominently beside the pavement.

> Th Santiphap: car parts and other automotive gear make this the place for kicking tyres.

## 👁 SEE

Chinatown is all about temples and markets – both of which are spectacles of busy bodies and cramped labyrinths.

### ◎ HANG SURA LAO NGI CHUN

☎ 0 2221 8384; 123 Th Phra Ram IV; ⏰ 10am-6pm; 🚇 Hualamphong; ♿
This antique apothecary specialises in the Chinese version of Popeye's can of spinach: herbal liquors that make the weak strong, the impotent virile and the elderly immortal. An assortment of the herbs used in the concoctions line the walls and regulars file in for a quick shot chased by a glass of water or tea.

### ◎ NAKHON KASEM

cnr Th Yaowarat & Th Chakrawat; ⏰ 8am-8pm; 🚤 Tha Saphan Phut
Cooking equipment, spare electronic parts, and other bits you didn't know could be resold are on hand at this open-air market. During looser times, this was known as the Thieves Market, selling the fruits of the five-finger discount.

### ◎ SRI GURUSINGH SABHA TEMPLE

cnr Th Chakraphet & Th Phahurat; donations accepted; ⏰ 9am-5pm; 🚌 506, 73, 🚤 Tha Saphan Phut; ♿
This sleek and modern Sikh temple (it's kitted out with elevators and marble throughout) is devoted to Guru Granth Sahib, one

of the last 10 gurus or teachers. You'll find it down a little alleyway off Th Chakraphet.

### TROK ITSARANUPHAP

**Trok Itsaranuphap; admission free;** 6am-6pm; Tha Ratchawong
Nudge your way deep into one of Chinatown's famous capillaries, where vendors sell dried goods, half-alive filleted fish and vats of unidentifiable pickled things. The *soi*'s poetic finale is lined with stalls selling elaborate funeral offerings and 'passports to heaven' that include paper houses and cars to take loved ones into the next life. You'll find all the action between Sampeng Lane (Soi Wanit 1) and Th Yommarat Sukhum.

### WAT MANGKON KAMALAWAT

**Th Charoen Krung; admission free, donations accepted;** 9am-6pm; 501, 507, 73, Tha Ratchawong
This Chinese temple is a labyrinth of vestibules. The gods of fortune in one of the first chambers is the most popular. Outside the temple, vendors sell heavenly food (oranges and steamed buns in the shape of lotus flowers) that are purchased as offerings. Located east of Th Ratchawong.

### WAT RATCHABOPHIT

**Th Atsadang; admission free, donations accepted;** 9am-6pm; 15, 53 Tha Tien; good
Commissioned by Rama V soon after he came to the throne, this beautiful temple is decorated with Chinese porcelain. European influences are reasonably strong, too – look at the uniforms of the carved guards on the door.

### WAT TRAIMIT

0 2225 9775; Th Traimit & Th Phra Ram IV; admission 20B; 8am-5pm; Hualamphong;
The Temple of the Golden Buddha sees a lot of visitors for one very big reason: the world's largest golden Buddha (5.5 tonnes and

Heavenly pursuits at Wat Mangkon Kamalawat

Weird and wonderful knick-knacks keep buyers and vendors bemused at Sampeng Lane Market

3m tall). An interesting minor attraction at the temple are the automated fortune telling machines; feed your money into the machine that corresponds to the day of the week you were born.

# 🛍 SHOP

## 🏠 JOHNNY'S GEMS *Jewellery*
☎ 0 2222 4065; 199 Th Feuang Nakhon; ⏲ 9.30am-6pm Mon-Sat; 🚌 508, 15, 🚢 Tha Tien; ♿
Johnny's is consistently recommended by expats, who return again and again for the reliable set jewellery and attentive service. They'll honestly point out the difference between costume and heirloom. Near Th Charoen Krung.

## 🏠 PAK KHLONG MARKET
*Market*
Th Chakkaphet; ⏲ 24hr; 🚢 Tha Ratchini; ♿
Get up early or stay out late to catch this 24-hour market, where the city stocks up on orchids, lilies and other tropical flowers. Pak Khlong is also one Bangkok's fresh fruit and veggie markets. Located near Tha Ratchini, Phahurat.

## 🏠 PHAHURAT MARKET *Market*
cnr Th Phahurat & Th Chakraphet; ⏲ 10am-9pm; 🚌 73, 🚢 Tha Saphan Phut
A confusing warren of shops and narrow lanes make up Little India's cloth and clothing market. You'll find saris, faux fur, bolts of fabric,

rowdy prints, Thai dance costumes and a heck of a lot of kids' stuff (pyjamas, jumpers, bibs). But you might not find your way out.

### 🖼 SAMPENG LANE MARKET
*Market*

**Sampeng Lane;** 🕑 **10am-10pm;** 🚌 **501, 507, 73,** 🚤 **Tha Ratchawong**
You can get anything you want in Sampeng Lane (or Soi Wanit 1) as long as you appreciate the concept of economies of scale. Sandals? Take a 12-pack. Inflatable Superman? They've got five for 400B. If you look hard, you'll find some shopfronts selling tea and tobacco, just like in the old days.

## 🍴 EAT
When you say 'Chinatown', Bangkokians reflexively start slurping noodles. The neighbouring district of Phahurat (or Little India), dishes up curries and samosas.

### 🍴 HONG KONG NOODLES
*Chinese*                               $

**136/4 Trok Itsaranuphap;** 🕑 **10am-8pm** 🚌 **507, 73,** 🚤 **Tha Ratchawong;** ♿
This crowded noodle shop delivers aromatic bowls of roasted duck noodles *(kǔaytǐaw pèt yâang)* with slippery won tons in a restorative broth. Located near the corner of Th Charoen Krung.

### 🍴 JAY PUY *Thai-Chinese*       $
☎ **081 850 9960; cnr Th Mangkorn & Th Charoen Krung;** 🕑 **4-9pm**
Inconspicuous to the point of being invisible, this lauded curry stall proves Bangkokian's dedication to food over setting. Here's the catch: Jay Puy has no tables, diners sit on plastic stools in the middle of the sidewalk braving heat, noise and even rain in the wet season. All for a thick and flavourful bowl of *kaeng kàrii*, a Chinese-style curry.

### 🍴 OLD SIAM PLAZA FOOD CENTRE *Thai Sweets*       $
**ground fl, Old Siam Plaza, cnr Th Phahurat & Th Triphet;** 🕑 **10am-5pm;** 🚌 **507, 73,** 🚤 **Tha Saphan Phut;** ♿ ♿
Beans, rice, tapioca, corn – Thais can turn seemingly savoury ingredients into extraordinarily sweet desserts. Peruse these transformations: *lûuk chúp* (miniature fruits made of beans) and *khànǒm bêuang* (taco-shaped pancakes filled with shredded coconut and golden threads of sweetened egg yolk).

### 🍴 ROYAL INDIA *North Indian* $$
☎ **0 2221 6565; 392/1 Th Chakraphet;** 🕑 **10am-10pm;** 🚌 **507, 73,** 🚤 **Tha Saphan Phut;** ♿ V
You are unsure as you go down the dark laneway and open an unmarked door. Inside, tables of men are deep in discussion while a voluptuously moustached

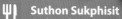
**Suthon Sukphisit**
*Author of Cornucopia, a weekly food column in the Bangkok Post*

**Best destination in Bangkok for eating?** Chinatown, because it has both good food and lots of atmosphere. **Best time to visit Chinatown?** Evening, because it's not hot, there's lots of food and the quality is very high – you won't be disappointed! **Favourite street stall in Chinatown?** Jay Puy (p77) is a curry stall that has no tables. People eat by holding the plate with their hand. During the rainy season this place has no roof or umbrellas, but people still go there. **One Thai dish visitors to Bangkok shouldn't miss?** Green curry. It's not too spicy, but it has spices, and is representative of Thai flavours

*By Austin Bush*

Indian man flogs golf clubs on cable TV. You soon discover that the food is incredible and the dhal indescribably delicious. Mission accomplished.

### 🍴 SHANGARILA Chinese $$-$$$

☎ 0 2224 5807; 206 Th Yaowarat; ⏲ 11am-10pm; 🚌 507, 73, 🚤 Tha Ratchawong; 🚶 V

Burned out on raucous Chinatown? Then duck into this air-con fuelling station for straightforward Thai-Chinese meals: *râat nâa* (stir-fried noodles in gravy) and grilled duck over rice. At weekends, it becomes more formal with multi-generational families arranged around Peking duck banquets.

### 🍴 SOI TEXAS SEAFOOD STALLS Chinese Seafood $$

Th Phadungdao; ⏲ 6-10pm; 🚌 507, 73, 🚤 Tha Ratchawong; 🚶 🚶

After the sun goes, this street (also known as Soi Texas) sprouts outdoor barbecues, iced seafood trays and footpath seating. People serving food dash every which way, cars plough through narrow streets, and before you know it you're tearing into a plate of grilled prawns like a starved alley cat. Blaring Chinese pop music and limbless beggars will make your visit an extra-surreal experience. Soi Texas is located off Th Yaowarat.

---

**GOING IT ALONE**

As a rule, Thais don't eat by themselves, after all, it would limit the number of dishes they can order. You may feel a bit uncomfortable at an upmarket restaurant by yourself, but you'll fit right in at noodle and curry shops and night markets, which dish up one-plate meals.

---

## ⭐ PLAY

### ☆ ABOUT STUDIO/ABOUT CAFE Art Space

☎ 0 2623 1742-3; 42-46 Th Maitrichit; ⏲ times vary; Ⓜ Hualamphong, 🚌 53; 🚶

This Chinatown storefront will lead you by the hand into deep-end modern-art appreciation: hip-hop, abstract art and poetry readings. Watch for openings and exhibits as hours vary.

### ☆ CHALERMKRUNG ROYAL THEATRE Theatre

☎ 0 2224 4499; cnr Th Charoen Krung & Th Triphet; 🚌 501, 507, 508, 🚤 Tha Saphan Phut; 🚶 🚶

This restored Thai Deco building, also known as Sala Chaloem Krung, hosts *khon* performances and modern Thai drama. Here *khon* is high-tech, with a flash audio system and computer-generated laser graphics. Dress respectfully (no shorts, sleeveless tops or sandals).

# >SIAM SQUARE, PRATUNAM & PLOENCHIT

If sprawling Bangkok were to have a centre, this would be it. Yet, no one calls it that. Instead locals refer to the various municipal districts or major roads to keep their mega capital in bite-size pieces. The Skytrain transit system, which sails along the backbone of modern Bangkok, has helped forge a sense of convergence and blocks of shopping malls have attached themselves to the stations like vacuum tubes leading directly into the stores. Amid this world of malls and office towers is an emerging fashion scene where disposing of income is serious business both for international visitors and local Thais.

Not all of old Bangkok has been erased by the boxy shopping centres. Pratunam (Water Gate) retains a squatty village identity alongside Khlong

## SIAM SQUARE, PRATUNAM & PLOENCHIT

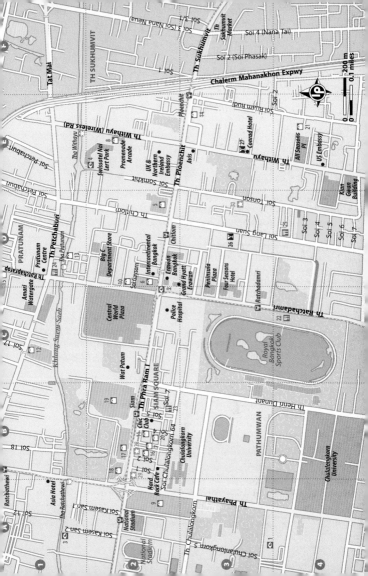

Saen Saeb and a dense everyday market. At night the exhaust-filled intersection of Th Phetchaburi and Th Ratchaprarop is a nucleus of outdoor dining, where families and friends are so absorbed by the meal that they ignore the capital's ever present noise and pollution.

# SEE

## CHULALONGKORN ART CENTRE

☎ 0 2218 2965; www.car.chula.ac.th; Centre of Academic Resources Bldg, 7th fl, Chulalongkorn University, Th Phayathai; 🕙 10am-7pm Mon-Fri; 🚇 Siam, 🚇 Samyan

Chula professors as well as major names in the Thai and international modern art scene are exhibited at this university museum. Permanent exhibits include Thai art retrospectives.

## ERAWAN SHRINE

cnr Th Ploenchit & Th Ratchadamri; admission free; 🕙 8am-7pm; 🚇 Chitlom; ♿

In BKK commerce and religion are not mutually exclusive. This Brahman shrine was built after accidents delayed construction of the first Erawan Hotel. News of the shrine's protective powers spread and merit makers now stream into the courtyard with their own petitions.

## JIM THOMPSON'S HOUSE

☎ 0 2216 7368; Soi Kasem San 2, Th Phra Ram I; admission 100/50B; 🕙 9am-5pm, compulsory tours in English & French every 10 min; 🚇 National Stadium, 🚌 508, 73, 🚤 khlong taxi to Tha Ratchathewi

An American expat living in Bangkok assembled this collection of Thai art and architecture that visitors can appreciate on daily tours. The guides are professional and knowledgeable about the former resident and Thai traditions. For more information see p21.

## LINGAM SHRINE

Nai Lert Park, Th Withayu; admission free; 🕙 8am-6pm; 🚤 khlong taxi to Tha Withayu; ♿

### ACCIDENT OR FOUL PLAY?

Jim Thompson's appreciation of Thai arts and crafts built a museum-worthy homestead as well as a successful silk business. But the cultural entrepreneur disappeared from his comfortable life under mysterious circumstances while visiting the Cameron Highlands, Malaysia in 1967. Some muse that Jim Thompson, a former CIA agent, was snatched by communist spies, while others swear he met his maker between the fangs of a man-eating tiger. Much less fascinating, but far more likely, is that he was run over by a Malaysian truck driver.

Lovingly selected art amid a luscious setting at Jim Thompson's House

This little shrine at the back of Swissotel Nai Lert Park was built for the spirit of a nearby tree. But soon word spread that the shrine had fertility powers and a small forest of wooden phalluses sprung up creating one of Bangkok's bawdiest shrines.

### ◉ SIAM OCEAN WORLD
☎ 0 2687 2000; www.siamoceanworld .co.th; basement, Siam Paragon, Th Phra Ram I; admission 450/280B; ☽ 9am-10pm; ⑧ Siam; ♿
Take the plunge into the underwater world of this massive aquarium. The little ones can visit the ocean depths in the glass-enclosed Deep Reef zone or view the daily feeding of penguins and sharks (which aren't invited to the same table).

## 🛍 SHOP
A visit to Bangkok's shopping malls is as important as the temple tours, and both invoke elements of the national character. Plus you can travel several kilometres of air-conditioning by weaving through the grove of shopping centres and the elevated walkways connecting to the Skytrain stations.

### 📖 ASIA BOOKS Books
☎ 0 2610 9609; 2nd fl, Siam Paragon, Th Phra Ram I; ☽ 10am-10pm; ⑧ Siam
One of the first English-language bookstores in Thailand, Asia Books continues to dominate the market with a wide selection of books and magazines. Also at Siam Discovery Center (p88) and the Emporium (p125).

NEIGHBOURHOODS

SIAM SQUARE, PRATUNAM & PLOENCHIT

## ☐ CENTRAL CHITLOM
*Shopping Centre*
☎ 0 2793 7000; 1027 Th Ploenchit; ☼ 10am-9pm; ⓡ Chitlom; ♿
In this internationally educated department store, executive-strength credit cards cruise the escalators thumbing homewares, *faràng*-sized (Westerner-sized) clothes and cosmetics.

## ☐ FLY NOW *Fashion*
☎ 0 2656 1359; 2nd fl, Gaysorn Plaza, cnr Th Ploenchit & Th Ratchadamri; ☼ 10am-9pm; ⓡ Chitlom; ♿
This Bangkok-born label has flown its flowing, feminine designs all the way to London and back (having opened at London Fashion Week twice) and still lands effortlessly on the daily runways of Bangkok's fashion elite. Also in Siam Paragon (p89).

## ☐ GAYSORN PLAZA
*Shopping Centre*
☎ 0 2656 1149; cnr Th Ploenchit & Th Ratchadamri; ☼ 10am-10pm; ⓡ Chitlom; ♿
When you think Gaysorn, you're mining for shoes or handbags. This fashion palace accommodates all the haughty international designers (Gucci, Prada, Louis Vuitton et al) plus Thai high-flyers (Fly Now and Senada), giving credibility to the city's self-endowed title, 'Fashion City'.

## ☐ JASPAL *Fashion*
☎ 0 2251 5918; 2nd fl, Siam Center, cnr Th Phayathai & Th Phra Ram I; ☼ 10am-9pm; ⓡ Siam; ♿
With a finger on the pulse of Western trends and a constant eye on the international fash mags, Jaspal is a high-street label for guys and girls not born in the silver-spoon league. Also at the Emporium (p126).

## ☐ JIM THOMPSON *Fashion*
Siam Paragon, Th Phra Ram I; ☼ 10am-9pm; ⓡ Siam
This is the newest outlet of the acclaimed Thai silk brand. Also on Th Surawong (p99) and at the Emporium (p126).

## ☐ KINOKUNIYA BOOKS *Books*
☎ 0 2610 9500; 3rd fl, Siam Paragon, Th Phra Ram I; ☼ 10am-10pm; ⓡ Siam; ♿
Bangkok will have to adopt some diligent reading habits to support this huge new bookstore in Siam Paragon. The English-language

### CALL ME LUCKY
Think telephone numbers are just a batch of digits to programme into your phone? In Thailand, a lucky telephone number is the key to success. On the 4th floor of MBK, telephone numbers with auspicious combinations (nines are golden) are sold off like antique collections.

## ALL THAT GLITTERS

Ah, the gem scam. We all know of someone who's been duped but still the Land of Smiles keeps relieving us of untold sums. Let the warning bells ring when a friendly local and/or fellow national approaches you and casually asks you along to their friend's gem (and/or tailoring) shop or a one-day-only sale. The gem scam usually ends with you being talked into buying low-grade unset gems and posting them home, where you'll find out they're worth very little. Just remember that the gem trade is a long and established industry that doesn't need your help in circumventing import regulations. A deal too good to be true almost certainly is.

options and magazines are endless. Also at the Emporium (p126).

### 🏠 LEA SILK Tailor

☎ 0 2252 0623; www.banrengkhai.com; 1st fl, Promenade Arcade, Raffles Nai Lert Park, 2/4 Th Withayu; 🕑 10am-6pm; 🚇 Chitlom; 🚌 62, 76, 🚤 khlong taxi to Tha Withayu; 🚻

Dutch-born textile artist Lea Laarakker Dingjan employs village women in the famed silk-weaving province of Surin to produce the jewel-toned fabric that she uses as a canvas for her striking modern designs. A percentage of the profits from her store is re-invested into the weaving communities.

### 🏠 MAE FAH LUANG Fashion

☎ 0 2658 0424; www.doitung.org; 4th fl, Siam Discovery Center, cnr Th Phayathai & Th Phra Ram I; 🕑 10am-9pm; 🚇 Siam; 🚻

Another handwoven tradition, these cotton textiles are produced as part of HRH the late Princess Mother's programme

to transition northern Thailand villages away from opium production. Bolts of fabric are sold alongside ready-to-wear women's designs that update this ethnic-hippie fabric into new millennium styles.

### 🏠 MAH BOON KRONG Shopping Centre

☎ 0 2620 9000; Th Phra Ram I & Th Phayathai; 🕑 10am-10pm; 🚌 508, 47, 73, 🚇 National Stadium; 🚻

Fast becoming Bangkok's most famous mall, MBK is an inside version of the Asian markets. You'll find lots of ordinary bargains as well as crowds of savvy shoppers. For more information, see p24.

### 🏠 NARAYANA PHAND Handicrafts

☎ 0 2252 4670; 127 Th Ratchadamri; 🕑 10am-9pm; 🚇 Chitlom, 🚤 khlong taxi to Tha Pratunam; 🚻

As a not-for-profit enterprise for distributing villagers' handicrafts, Narayana Phand has its heart

**Chamnan Pakdeesuk**
*Designer for clothing brand Fly Now*

**What's your favourite place to shop for clothes in Bangkok?** Along the side of Silom Rd (Map p95). I love the cheap T-shirts. **How does Bangkok influence your designs?** The tackiness of the city influences me; I know it's tacky, but I still want to use it. It's in my blood. **What are some Thai brands to look out for?** Good Mixer is nice. It has a holiday feel to it. For something more cool there's Greyhound, although it can be a bit too stylish. **What is the Bangkok look?** It's a cross between American, European and Asian styles, plus the casualness due to the weather. **What are some clothes shopping destination visitors shouldn't miss:** Siam Center (p88) and Siam Square (p89). There are lots of Thai designers and you can find everything: casual, dressy, sportswear.

*By Austin Bush*

in the right place, although it feels a bit like a souvenir factory. Regardless, the gaudy souvenirs are handy.

### NEW DJ SIAM *Music*
☎ 0 22251 2513; 292/16 Siam Square, Soi 4; ⏱ 10am-5pm; 🚇 Siam; ♿
In the heart of teen-landia, this tiny store feeds the kiddies with the hottest overseas alt-options as well as all the Thai-bred indie groups.

### PANTA *Décor*
☎ 0 2658 0415; www.pantathailand .com; 4th fl, Siam Discovery Center, Th Phra Ram I; ⏱ 10am-9pm; 🚇 Siam
After years of pressboard, Bangkok finally has contemporary options in home décor and furnishings. The leader of the movement is Panta, whose award-winning designs use local products, crafts-manship and sensibilities that won't fit in a suitcase but would look great in a city loft. Also at Siam Paragon (p89).

### PANTIP PLAZA
*Shopping Centre*
Th Phetchaburi; ⏱ 10am-8pm; 🚌 505, 511, 512, 🚢 Tha Pratunam
For the time being Pantip is the Wild West of computer components. Discounted pirated software, fresh off the factory con-veyor belts, is the primary draw turning obedient citizens into reckless law-breakers. Hardware junkies work the floors for used parts to beef up ailing machines.

### PAPAYA FURNITURE *Décor*
☎ 0 2655 3335; www.design-athome .com; Th Ratchadamri; ⏱ 10am-6pm; 🚇 Chitlom 🚢 Tha Pratunam
Furniture and lamps are stocked up to the rafters of this re-sale warehouse. You'll find mostly mod bits with a dash of kitsch and a few requisite Buddhas, but a wander through the overstuffed rooms will suit thrift-store junkies. To get there, take the second *soi* after the Big C on Th Ratchadamri and fol-low the car park ramp on the left.

### THE ELECTRONICS MYTH
Somewhere in cyberspace or by word of mouth, folks got the crazy idea that Bangkok is a mecca for cheap electronics. Because we care, here is the truth: digital cameras, laptops, and other new gadgets are going to cost you the same or more in Bangkok than back home. Where techies do win is in Bangkok's still untamed frontier for intellectual property. Despite pressures on Thai officials for IP enforcement, everyone's favourite contraband, pirated soft-ware and music, is outrageously cheap in the Land of Knock-Offs.

Escalators to shopping heaven, Siam Paragon

### 🖰 PINKY TAILORS *Tailor*
☎ 0 2253 6328; 888/40 Th Ploenchit;
🕙 10am-8pm Mon-Sat; 🚇 Chitlom
Custom-made suit jackets are Mr
Pinky's specialty. He also has a
quiet, no-hassle shop where you
can touch all of the fabrics without
stumbling over a sales associate.
Behind the Mahatun Building.

### 🖰 PRATUNAM MARKET *Market*
cnr Th Phetchaburi & Th Ratchaprarop;
🕙 10am-9pm; 🚌 505, 511, 512,
🚢 khlong taxi to Tha Pratunam
A common folk market, Pratunam
sells a bit of everything and is the
best stop for an extra piece of

luggage, an umbrella or Cookie
Monster slippers.

### 🖰 PROPAGANDA *Décor*
☎ 0 2664 8574; 2nd fl, Siam Discovery
Center, cnr Th Phayathai & Th Phra
Ram I; 🕙 10am-8pm; 🚇 National
Stadium or Siam; 🔥
If Propaganda is truly trying to
live up to its name, then count
us as officially indoctrinated. It's
hard to resist the charms of this
fun, stark-white shop with all
sorts of functional design pieces
created by Thai designers, such as
Chaiyut Plypetch's lamps featuring
the anatomically cartoonish Mr
P. There's another Propaganda
branch in the Emporium (p127)
shopping centre.

### 🖰 SIAM CENTER & SIAM
### DISCOVERY CENTER
*Shopping Centre*
☎ 0 2658 1000-19; cnr Th Phayathai &
Th Phra Ram I; 🕙 10am-9pm; 🚇 Siam;
🔥 good
These sister centres fill in the
budget range between proletariat
Mah Boon Krong and luxe Siam
Paragon. The Discovery Center has
a little bit of everything, but mainly
stylish home-furnishing stores.
Follow the pouty, mobile-phone
crowd to link with Siam Center,
which has recently been rebrand-
ed for the younger set with more
fashion and thumping techno.

### SIAM PARAGON
*Shopping Centre*

☎ 0 2610 8000; www.siamparagon
.co.th; Th Phra Ram I; ⏱ 10am-10pm;
🚇 Siam; ♿

A shopper could dive in and never resurface in this airport-sized mall dedicated mainly to a Milky Way of famous luxury brands. More popular is the lobby atrium, referred to by some Thais as their new park, and the basement-level Gourmet Paradise (p90). If you collect trivia, this is allegedly the biggest mall in Southeast Asia.

### SIAM SQUARE
*Shopping Centre*

Th Phra Ram I; ⏱ most stores 10am-9pm; 🚇 Siam

The closest Bangkok comes to a boutique district is the open-air shopping complex, near the inter-section of Th Phayathai, known as Siam Square. This is ground-zero for youth fashion, wedged between MBK and Chulalongkorn University. Closet-sized boutiques line Soi 2, 3 and 4. Some of the winners include: **September** ( ☎ 0 1815 8641; Soi 3, Siam Square), **AB-Normal** ( ☎ 0 2658 3884; 352, room 21, under Siam Theater) and **It's Happened to Be a Closet** ( ☎ 0 2985 9345; 266/3 Soi 3, Siam Square).

### UTHAI'S GEMS *Jewellery*

☎ 0 2253 8582 28/7 Soi Ruam Rudi, Th Ploenchit; ⏱ 10am-6pm Mon-Sat; 🚇 Ploenchit

Uthai's Gems showroom is in quiet Soi Ruam Rudi serving the discriminating embassy community. Non-hagglers appreciate his fixed prices and good service. Appointments reccommended.

### VIP DINING

Although Thai meals appear very informal there are many subtle gestures of honour and communal gestures extended to guests and elders. Most Thais will pick out the most delicious pieces of a whole fish and serve it to their guest (that typically means you) or make sure that you receive spoonfuls of dishes too far away to reach yourself. Also notice that the person closest to the drink bottles or the serving dish of rice becomes the de facto server, loading up everyone else before plunging in themselves. To show your appreciation for the meal, leave a little rice on your plate to signal satiation.

The communal spirit of a Thai meal is even more apparent when eating the kingdom's famous curries *(kaeng)* and soups (such as *tôm yam kûng*). Both arrive at the table in a single bowl from which diners ladle for each other the contents into an individual bowl and then spoon the edible bits on to rice. Not everything in a *tôm yam* can be eaten; if it is hard to chew, then you've discovered the Thai version of bay leaves. After sharing a Thai meal, our Western manners might seem a tad selfish.

# ⊓⊔ EAT

From mall munching to causes célèbres, Siam Square and nearby Th Ploenchit, Th Ratchadamri and Th Withayu offer a full house of eating options.

## ⊓⊔ 100 RATCHADAMRI
*Thai & Italian*          $$$
☎ 0 2251 1705; Royal Bangkok Sports Club, 100 Th Ratchadamri; ⏰ 6-11pm; 🚇 Ratchadamri; ♿

Well-known in blue-blood circles, this restaurant occupies a prestigious location on the grounds of the Royal Bangkok Sports Club. But cast aside visions of bird-dog oil paintings, rather, this place sports a nightclub setting (sans the decibels) and outdoor banquettes facing the club greens. True to the educated-abroad palate, there is a Thai and Italian menu. *Yam sôm oh puu* (pomelo salad with deep-fried crab) earns a hole-in-one.

## ⊓⊔ BAAN KHUN MAE *Thai*   $$
☎ 0 2658 4112; Soi 7, Siam Square; ⏰ 11am-10pm; 🚇 Siam; ♿ 👶 Ⓥ

Welcome to Mama's House, a homey little spot for respectable Thai food at hospitable prices. Order till your heart's content and try all the dishes you've never heard of, because the final bill won't wound your adventurousness.

## ⊓⊔ FOODLOFT *International*   $$
☎ 0 2655 7777; 7th fl, Central Chitlom, Th Ploenchit; ⏰ 10am-9pm; 🚇 Chitlom; ♿ 👶 Ⓥ

Soaking in a view can just as easily be matched with slurping down noodles as it can with mincing your meal. Amid this industrial-chic cafeteria, city views dominate the dining room while shoppers refuel with local and international options.

## ⊓⊔ GOURMET PARADISE
*Thai & International*       $$
☎ 0 2610 8000; ground fl, Siam Paragon, Th Phra Ram I; ⏰ 10am-9pm; 🚇 Siam; ♿ 👶 Ⓥ

One entire floor is dedicated to food and eating in Siam Paragon's ubermall universe. The feudal divisions of Thai society are in full effect at weekends. The aristocrats file into the branches of successful white-linen restaurants, while the working class hustles through the food court with trays of noodles and stir-fries.

## ⊓⊔ GREYHOUND CAFE
*International*             $$$
☎ 0 2255 6965; Central Chitlom, 3rd fl, Th Ploenchit; ⏰ 11am-9pm; 🚇 Chitlom

Affiliated with the Thai clothing brand, this is one of several cafés to nourish peckish shoppers. Also at the Emporium (p131).

## FOOD WITHOUT THE FUMES

Shopping centre food courts are usually examples of food abuse, but Bangkok's food courts retain the same dedication to flavours as their streetside brethren and without the noise or heat. All the shopping centres have one, but MBK's food centre, Siam Paragon's Gourmet Paradise and Central Chitlom's Foodloft are genre stand outs. The process works like this: first you buy coupons or a debit card from a designated booth and use this intermediary currency to buy food. A refund for any unspent money is available on the day of purchase.

### 🍴 MBK FOOD COURT
*Thai-Chinese* $

**6th fl, MBK shopping centre, cnr Th Phra Ram I & Th Phayathai;** 🕐 **10am-10pm;** 🚇 **National Stadium;** ♿ 👶 Ⓥ
It's a lot like having all your favourite street food vendors in one place. There is no need to visit the noodle woman in one street, the fruit juice man in another and then hike to find a mango and sticky rice stall. Come early for the popular vegetarian stall.

### 🍴 PRATUNAM CHICKEN RICE RESTAURANTS *Thai* $

**cnr Th Phetchaburi & Th Ratchaprarop;** 🕐 **7pm-4am;** 🚕 **taxi;** 👶
At the Pratunam intersection are two competing *khâo man kài* (sliced steamed chicken served over rice) restaurants known by every taxi driver in the city (just say 'Midnight Kai Ton' to get here). Folks argue about which one is better, but we vote for the shop further from the corner. The dipping sauce with big chunks of ginger is its bird in the hand.

### 🍴 WHOLE EARTH RESTAURANT *Thai Vegetarian* $$

☎ **0 2252 5574; 93/3 Soi Lang Suan;** 🕐 **11.30am-2pm & 5.30-11pm;** 🚇 **Chitlom;** ♿ 👶 Ⓥ
You might come to feel like you're spending a long afternoon in your New Age auntie's lounge room, which she has decorated with souvenirs from the 'getting spiritual' tour of Asia she undertook in the 1970s. And, if you stop to think about it, the vegetarian food is a bit like that too – homey, familiar and nutritious, but not actually all that exciting. Except for the divine fruit lassis.

## 🍸 DRINK

### 🍸 CAFÉ TRIO *Bar*

☎ **0 252 6572; 36/11-12 Soi Lang Suan, Th Ploenchit;** 🕐 **6pm-midnight Mon-Sat;** 🚇 **Ploenchit**
Café Trio meets so few strangers that it is expected for you to introduce yourself upon arrival. Patti is the mistress of ceremonies and will make sure you drink more

NEIGHBOURHOODS

SIAM SQUARE, PRATUNAM & PLOENCHIT

Go underwater without getting wet at Siam Ocean World (p83)

than you intended. Her subjects, a regular crowd of diplomats and professionals, are happy to toast her every whim.

### ▼ DIPLOMAT BAR *Bar*
☎ 0 2690 9999; Conrad Hotel, 87 Th Withayu; ◐ 6pm-midnight; 🚇 Ploenchit
Young sophisticates toast their good fortune and good looks at one of Bangkok's leading hotel bars. The bubbly and the grapey spirits are the tipples of choice while the diva-led lounge band serenades.

## ⭐ PLAY
When it is hot and steamy outside, Bangkok's plush cinemas are a welcome escape. Dozens of theatres screen movies in English, with Thai subtitles; check the *Bangkok Post* or www.movieseer.com for

session times. Tickets cost around 150B for basic seating and up to 600B for VIP. The royal anthem is played before every screening and patrons are expected to stand respectfully.

### ⭐ EGV GRAND *Cinema*
☎ 0 2812 9999; 6th fl, Siam Discovery Center, Th Phra Ram I; 🚇 Siam; ♿ 🚼
Place your snack order on the way in, wait until after the royal anthem to recline your sofa chair to horizontal and snuggle in for the long haul. Try not to fall asleep before your food arrives.

### ⭐ KRUNG SRI IMAX *Cinema*
☎ 0 2511 5555; Siam Paragon, Th Phra Ram I; admission 600/250B; 🚇 Siam; ♿ 🚼
Be engulfed by the big screen technology of IMAX at this sparkly new theatre. Screenings range from nature features of audience-hunting

**WHICH WAY TO TOLLYWOOD?**
If you've got your eye on the silver screen, Thailand is emerging as an art-movie darling. Bangkok's International Film Festival (p30) screens Thai talent, as do art house cinemas such as **Lido** ( ☎ 0 2252 6498; Siam Square, Th Phra Ram I; 🚇 Siam), **Scala** ( ☎ 0 2251 2861; Siam Square Soi 1, Th Phra Ram I; 🚇 Siam) and **House** (Map pp140–1; ☎ 0 2641 5177; UMG Building, RCA/Royal City Avenue, near Th Petchaburi; 🚇 Petburi).

sharks to special-effects versions of Hollywood action flicks.

⭐ **PARAGON CINEPLEX** *Cinema*
☎ 0 2515 5555; Siam Paragon, Th Phra Ram I; 🚇 Siam; ♿ 👶
Designed to outdo everyone, Siam Paragon's theatre has better seats (more accurately beds), more showtimes and bigger screens. Capitalism at its best.

⭐ **SF CINEMA CITY** *Cinema*
☎ 0 2611 6444; 7th fl, Mah Boon Krong, cnr Th Phra Ram I & Th Phayathai; 🚇 National Stadium; ♿ 👶
Grab a big box of popcorn and find a seat among the Thai teenagers waiting to see the latest blockbuster. If that sounds like a nightmare, spend the extra cash and buy one of the gold-class seats.

⭐ **SF CITY BOWL** *Bowling*
☎ 0 2611 7171; 7th fl, Mah Boon Krong, cnr Th Phra Ram I & Th Phayathai; from 30B; 🕙 10am-1am; 🚇 National Stadium; ♿
Thai teenagers crowd this psychedelically decorated bowling alley

at all hours of the day and night. The cost varies, depending what time you play.

⭐ **SPA 1930** *Spa*
☎ 0 2254 8606; www.spa1930.com; Soi Tonson, Th Ploenchit; à la carte from 1200B, packages from 3800B; 🕙 9.30am-9.30pm; 🚇 Chitlom; ♿
Discreet and sophisticated, Spa 1930 rescues relaxers from the contrived spa ambience of New Age music and ingredients you'd rather see at a dinner party. The menu is simple (face, body care and body massage) and the scrubs and massage oils are logical players.

⭐ **THANN SANCTUARY** *Spa*
☎ 0 2658 0550; www.thann.info; 5th fl, Siam Discovery Center; 🕙 10am-9pm; 🚇 Siam; ♿ good
First you'll be lured in for a sniff test of Thann & Harnn's all-natural, locally developed body-care products. Lemon grass, lime, rosemary, all smell good enough to eat. Around the corner from the shop is the spa centre for post-shopping therapy.

# >RIVERSIDE & SILOM

Swollen ships dispensed exotic goods and explorers on the riverside docks that once defined Bangkok's early port. Remnants of this era are preserved along the little lanes that wind through abandoned warehouses and crumbling neoclassical palaces facing the river. The new kings of the river are the luxury riverside hotels that drink in the watery and romantic view. Tucked in between are Muslim and Indian communities that replaced the old European mercantile class.

As the modern era nudged out shipping, business migrated inland along Bangkok's financial district of Th Silom. During the week, the streets

## RIVERSIDE & SILOM

### ○ SEE
Holy Rosary Church ........ 1 B1
Kathmandu Photo
Gallery .......................... 2 D3
MR Kukrit Pramoj House 3 F4
Queen Saovabha
Memorial Institute Snake
Farm ............................. 4 F1
Robot Building ............. 5 E4
Sri Mariamman Temple.. 6 D3

### ⬛ SHOP
H Gallery ....................... 7 E3
House of Chao ............... 8 D2
House of Gems .............. 9 B3
Jim Thompson ............ 10 F1
Lin Silvercraft ............. 11 B3
Maison des Arts .......... 12 B4
Motif & Maris .............. 13 C3
Old Maps & Prints ..... (see 16)
Patpong Night
Market ......................... 14 F2
Plan Creations ........... 15 E3
River City ..................... 16 B1
Silom Village Trade
Centre ......................... 17 D3
Soi Lalai Sap Market..... 18 E3
SV Jewellery ................ 19 B3

Thai Home Industries...20 B3
Thavibu Gallery ............ 21 C3

### 🍴 EAT
Ban Chiang ................... 22 C3
Bussaracum .................. 23 D3
Circle of Friends ........... 24 E3
Eat Me ......................... 25 F3
Harmonique .................. 26 B2
Indian Hut ................... 27 C2
Kalpapruek
Restaurant .................. 28 D3
Kozo Sushi .................... 29 F2
Le Lys .......................... 30 F4
Le Normandie .......... (see 32)
Mizu's Kitchen ............. 31 F2
Oriental Hotel's
Author's Lounge ..........32 B3
Sara-Jane's .................. 33 F4
Soi Pradit (Soi 20)
Market ......................... 34 D3
Somboon Seafood ....... 35 E2
Taling Pling ................. 36 D3
Tongue Thai ................. 37 B3
Wan Fah Cruises ....... (see 16)
Yok Yor Marina &
Restaurant .................. 38 A2

### ▼ DRINK
Balcony Bar .................. 39 F2
Bamboo Bar .............. (see 32)
O'Reilly's ...................... 40 F2
Sirocco & Sky Bar ........ 41 C3
Tapas .......................... 42 F2
Telephone .................... 43 F2
Three Sixty .................. 44 A2
V9 ............................... 45 D2

### ★ PLAY
Blue Elephant
Cooking School ............ 46 C4
DJ Station .................... 47 F1
Epicurean Kitchen ........ 48 F2
Fortune Tellers ............. 49 F1
Freeman ...................... 50 F2
Healthland Spa &
Massage ...................... 51 E3
Lucifer ......................... 52 F2
Oriental Hotel Spa,
Cooking Centre & Sala
Rim Naam .................... 53 A3
Ruen-Nuad Massage.... 54 F3
Sala Rim Naam ......... (see 32)
Silom Thai Cooking
School .......................... 55 D3
Silom Village ............... 56 D3

are packed with office workers en route to lunch stalls or business meetings while blind troubadours hope for spare bits of their lunch money. The crush of bodies makes Western cities look like sleepy villages. Unless you've come with briefcase in tow, you'll meet Silom at night thanks to the infamous red light district of Patpong, now a tamer skin circus and souvenir market.

# 👁 SEE

Sightseeing is limited in these parts, but the lanes between the river and Th Charoen Krung are good candidates for wandering. Th Silom used to be the outskirts of the city, evidenced by the European and Chinese cemeteries around Soi 11.

## 📷 KATHMANDU PHOTO GALLERY

☎ 0 2234 6700 87 Th Pan; 🕐 11am-7pm Tue-Sun; 🚇 Chong Nonsi
Manit Sriwanichpoom, one of Bangkok's leading photographers has opened his own gallery in a refurbished Chinese-style shophouse. Rotating exhibits by friends and peers are featured in the upstairs gallery, while the downstairs space is dedicated to the owner's portfolio.

## 🏛 MR KUKRIT PRAMOJ HOUSE

☎ 0 2286 8185; Soi 7, Th Narathiwat Ratchanakharin; admission 50B; 🕐 10am-5pm Sat & Sun; 🚇 Chong Nonsi
Author and statesman Mom Ratchawong Kukrit Pramoj once resided in this charming complex now open to the public. European-educated but devoutly Thai, MR Kukrit surrounded himself with the best of both worlds: five traditional teak buildings, Thai art, Western books and lots of heady conversations. A guided tour is recommended for a more intimate introduction to the former resident, who authored more than 150 books and served as prime minister of Thailand.

## 🐍 QUEEN SAOVABHA MEMORIAL INSTITUTE SNAKE FARM

☎ 0 2252 0161; cnr Th Phra Ram IV & Th Henri Dunant; admission 70B; 🕐 8.30am-4.30pm Mon-Fri, 8.30am-noon Sat & Sun, shows 11am & 2.30pm Mon-Fri, 11am Sat & Sun ; 🚇 Sala Daeng 🚇 Samyen; ♿
This snake farm, one of only a few worldwide, was established in 1923 to breed snakes for antivenins. The snake shows are a nice sideline, where snake handlers educate and freak out visitors about snakes by letting the baddest ones loose (don't fret, you're safe in the stands).

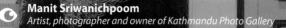

**Manit Sriwanichpoom**
*Artist, photographer and owner of Kathmandu Photo Gallery*

**A good area of Bangkok to take photos?** Silom Rd. It's easy to see the contrast between traditional and modern lifestyles there. **Tips for photography in Bangkok?** Bangkok is great for candid photography. There's always something happening, and you don't have to be a pro or have a good camera to capture it. **Favourite art gallery in Bangkok?** The Chulalongkorn University Art Centre (p82) has great contemporary art exhibitions. **Strengths of the Thai art scene?** Thais are great at style and design. **Weaknesses?** We are a non-confrontational culture and are reluctant to criticise through art.

By Austin Bush

NEIGHBOURHOODS

RIVERSIDE & SILOM

## WORTH THE TRIP

Bangkok has many full-fledged attractions but some of the most memorable sights are purely accidental. Here is a list of our favourites.

> Watching the cool kids hang-out in Siam Square (Map p81, B2)
> Joining the sweating-to-techno aerobics classes at Lumphini (p114) or Santichaiprakan Park (p56)
> Ogling the luxury cars in the 2nd-floor showroom at Siam Paragon (p89)
> Catching a commissioned dance at Lak Meuang (p46) or Erawan Shrine (p82)

### ⚙ ROBOT BUILDING

**cnr Th Sathon Tai & Soi Pikun; ☾ closed to the public; 🚇 Surasak**

During the crazy '80s, when no building project was too outlandish or expensive, architect Sumet Jumsai created his now-famous 'robot building' for the Bank of Asia (now owned by United Overseas Bank). Few were keen on it at the time, but now it seems quaint and retro. It is best viewed from the Surasak Skytrain platform.

### ⚙ SRI MARIAMMAN TEMPLE

**cnr Th Pan & Th Silom; donations accepted; ☾ 6am-8pm; 🚇 Chong Nonsi; ♿**

Thai Buddhism still honours its mother religion of Hinduism. Built by Tamil immigrants in the 1860s, this Hindu temple is a colourful place of worship in every sense of the word, from the multi-hued main temple to the eclectic range of people of many faiths and ethnicities who come to make offerings. Thais call it Wat Phra Si Maha Umathewi.

## 🛍 SHOP

The majority of Bangkok's antique stores congregate near their potential customers on Th Charoen Krung, near the riverside hotels.

### 🏠 H GALLERY *Gallery*

**☎ 0 1310 4428; www.hgallerybkk.com; Soi 12, Th Sathon; ☾ noon-6pm Thu-Sat, by appointment Sun-Wed; 🚇 Chong Nonsi, 🚌 17, 22**

H is a conduit for aspiring abstract artists deemed worthy enough to percolate into its New York gallery. Before jettisoning off to the Big Apple, most shows grace the walls of this neo-colonial gallery or Eat Me restaurant (p103).

### 🏠 HOUSE OF CHAO *Antiques*

**☎ 0 2635 7188; 9/1 Th Decho; ☾ 10am-6pm; 🚌 504, 15; ♿**

Dusty old antique shops littered with precious and not-so-precious junk are rare in Bangkok, but this spot is haphazardly filled with teak treasures from Thailand and Burma.

### 🖼 HOUSE OF GEMS *Antiques*

**1218 Th Charoen Krung;** 🕐 **10am-6pm Mon-Sat;** 🚌 **504, 75,** ⚓ **Tha Oriental**

The name 'House of Gems' is an interesting sales pitch for a shop claiming to sell dinosaur droppings. If you look in the window, dry cross-sections will teach you the subtle difference between the 'gems' of a carnivorous dinosaur, compared to its herbivorous friends. Don't say we didn't tell you that there's nothing you can't buy in Bangkok. Located near Th Surawong.

### 🖼 JIM THOMPSON *Fashion*

☎ **0 2632 8100 www.jimthompson.com; 9 Th Surawong;** 🕐 **9am-6pm;** 🚇 **Sala Daeng,** Ⓜ **Silom**

As you'd expect of the company that resurrected the Thai silk industry, you get nothing but impeccable fabric here. You can buy silk by the metre (which can be tailored onsite), silk scarves and neckties and accessories (including tablecloths, throw pillows and napkins). Jim Thompson stores are also located at the Emporium (p126) and Siam Paragon (p84) shopping centres.

### 🖼 LIN SILVERCRAFT *Jewellery*

☎ **0 2235 2108; 14 Soi 40, Th Charoen Krung;** 🕐 **10am-8pm;** 🚇 **Saphan Taksin,** 🚌 **504, 75,** ⚓ **Tha Oriental;** ♿

Lin might be a bit pricier than your average Bangkok silver shop but you know you're getting the genuine article. You can pick up classic pieces such as silver chokers, thick bangles and custom-engraved cuff links.

### 🖼 MAISON DES ARTS *Handicrafts*

☎ **0 2233 6297; 1334 Th Charoen Krung;** 🕐 **11am-6pm Mon-Sat;** 🚇 **Saphan Taksin,** 🚌 **504, 75,** ⚓ **Tha Oriental**

Hand-hammered, stainless steel tableware haphazardly occupies this warehouse retail shop. The bold style of the flatware dates back centuries and the staff applies no pressure to indecisive shoppers.

### TAXING STUFF INDEED

You can claim back some of the VAT (value-added tax) you've paid but the requirements are a little tricky. To qualify, you must have spent at least 5000B on the goods, which must be bought at participating stores, where you have to show your passport and complete the appropriate forms. You also must have been in Thailand for fewer than 180 days in a calendar year, be leaving the country by plane and apply for a refund with goods in hand at the airport departure hall. See the VAT Refund for Tourists website (www.rd.go.th/vrt/howwill.html) to make sense of it all.

Ferries sitting pretty on Mae Nam Chao Phraya (p12)

### ◻ MOTIF & MARIS *Handicrafts*

☎ 0 2635 9111; 296/7 Th Silom;
🕙 10am-8pm; 🚌 504, 76; ♿

It's rare to find someone in the rag trade still dedicated to the old arts of embroidery and smocking, so Motif & Maris is a surprise. Every piece of children's clothing hanging in this little shop is intricate and exquisite. The handmade soft toys and nursery accessories are pretty gorgeous, too. Also at the River City shopping complex (opposite).

### ◻ OLD MAPS & PRINTS
*Antiques*

☎ 0 2237 0077/8; www.classicmaps .com; 4th fl, River City, Th Yotha;
🕙 11am-7pm; 🚌 504, 75, 🚢 Tha Si Phraya; ♿

You could poke around in this shop for hours, flipping through the maps of Siam and Indochina, laughing at early explorers' quaint drawings of 'the natives' and sighing with delight at the exquisite framed prints.

### ◻ PATPONG NIGHT MARKET
*Market*

Soi 1 & 2, Th Silom; 🕙 6pm-2am;
🚇 Sala Daeng, ⊖ Silom

The Patpong area is the ultimate Bangkok cliché where everything can be had for a price. In one corner are the famous circus-like sex shows and in the other is a crowded market selling name brand knock-offs . (Make sure you bargain hard as prices are grossly inflated). And lying in ambush are the 'DVD, CVD, Sex' video sellers who pop up just as your wife has stepped past.

## PLAN CREATIONS
*Handicrafts*

☎ 0 2236 9410; www.plantoys.com; 114/1 Soi 10, Th Sathon; 🕒 10am-6pm Mon-Fri, 10am-4pm Sat; 🚇 Chong Nonsi; ♿ fair

If Lego went organic, you'd have a pretty close approximation of Plan Creations' imaginative wooden toys, made from rubber trees. To fill that lingering Christmas list, there are blocks, pull-along alligators and play sets (such as Noah's Ark and all the critters) targeted at children aged three to 10.

## RIVER CITY *Shopping centre*

☎ 0 2237 0077; Th Yotha; 🕒 10am-10pm; 🚌 504, 75, 🚤 Tha Si Phraya; ♿

Only got time for one antique shop? This four-floor complex of art, antiques and auctioneers is a one-stop shop for a Burmese Buddha image, black silk or a *benjarong* (traditional royal Thai ceramics) tea-set, and you pay for the quality. The stores can arrange

to ship your buys back home. Located off Th Charoen Krung.

## SILOM VILLAGE TRADE CENTRE *Handicrafts*

286 Th Silom; 🕒 10am-9pm; 🚇 Chong Nonsi; 🚌 504, 15; ♿

It's blissfully easy to wander around this cluster of shops. While some vendors sell the ubiquitous touristy fare, the antique shops have carved teak wall decorations to turn your house into a traditional Thai home.

## SOI LALAI SAP MARKET
*Market*

Soi 5, Th Silom; 🕒 10am-3pm Mon-Fri; 🚇 Chong Nonsi, 🚌 16, 36; ♿

Literally 'the *soi* that melts your money away', at lunchtime this street is packed with Thai secretaries bargaining for fake handbags, homewares and polyester clothing. Rejects from brand-name factories in Cambodia sometimes make an appearance here.

### FAKING IT
Knocking off name-brand goods is a Bangkok specialty. Many say that these fakes are after-hours creations: once the factory officially closes, the machines keep going to feed the underground market. These name-brands without quality control are the cream of the knock-off crop, while others are just copy-cats. It's all highly illegal, of course, and many Western manufacturers have long been pressuring the Thai government to get these goods off the street. But the grey market is tenacious at circumventing spotty enforcement. Now vendors only show off pictures of fake Rolexes to customers and once a deal has been sealed a runner delivers the goods in discreet packaging. The obvious similarities between buying drugs and fakes is often lost on the upright citizens admiring their new wristwatches.

NEIGHBOURHOODS

RIVERSIDE & SILOM

### ☐ SV JEWELLERY *Jewellery*

☎ 0 2233 7347; 1254-6 Th Charoen Krung; ⏱ 10am-5pm Mon-Sat; 🚇 Saphan Taksin, 🚌 504, 75, ⚓ Tha Oriental; ♿

With a big showroom on bustling Th Charoen Krung, SV Jewellery isn't just a shop for girly baubles and body decorations. You'll find cuff links in all sizes, shapes and attitudes, silver elephants, enormous gleaming photo frames and key rings.

### ☐ THAI HOME INDUSTRIES *Handicrafts*

☎ 0 2234 1736; 35 Soi Oriental, Th Charoen Krung; ⏱ 10am-8pm; 🚌 504, 75, ⚓ Tha Oriental; ♿

You can wander at will around this enormous traditional Thai building overflowing with boxes. The staff leaves you to your own devices to poke around the bronzeware, silverware (especially cutlery) and basketry.

### ☐ THAVIBU GALLERY *Gallery*

☎ 0 2266 5454; www.thavibu.com; 91 9/1 Th Silom, 3rd fl, Silom Galleria; ⏱ 11am-7pm Tue-Sat, noon-6pm Sun; 🚌 504, 15, 76; ♿

Young artists from Southeast Asia (namely Burma, Thailand and Vietnam) are showcased in this virtual and brick-and-mortar gallery. With a huge internet presence, Thavibu cultivates a wide international audi-

ence and is a major resource of art and art information for the region.

## 🍴 EAT

Bangkok's financial district does a lot of wining and dining, especially geared towards visiting tourists and businesspeople.

### 🍴 BAN CHIANG *Thai* $$

☎ 0 2236 7045; 14 Soi Si Wiang, Th Surasak; ⏱ 11am-2pm & 5-10.30pm; 🚇 Surasak; ♿

Don't expect to dive off the tourist trail at this foreigner friendly restaurant. Nonetheless the atmospheric wooden house and honest dishes will delight even the cynics.

### 🍴 BUSSARACUM *Thai* $$$

☎ 0 2266 6312; Sethiwan Tower, 139 Soi Pan, Th Silom; ⏱ 11am-2pm & 5-10.30pm; 🚌 504

Recipes once reserved for royalty are made available to all at Bussaracum (pronounced *boot-sa-ra-kam*). Intricate dishes and curry

### LOVE HURTS

Be careful before you start falling in love with images or statues of Buddha and other deities. For any image that isn't an amulet (intended for religious purposes), you'll need an export licence to take the object out of the country. Contact the National Museum on ☎ 0 2224 1370 for more application information.

pastes made from scratch are presented so much like works of art that it (almost) breaks your heart to dig a spoon into your delicate purple dumpling flowers and dramatically carved squash overflowing with seafood.

### 🍴 CIRCLE OF FRIENDS *Thai* $$
☎ 0 2237 0080; Soi 10, Th Sathorn; 🕙 11.30am-3pm; 🚇 Surasak or Chong Nonsi; 🚻 🛗
This unpretentious café shares space with Saeng-Arom Ashram and exudes a gentle tranquillity that self-help books champion. There are lots of veggie options and all the Thai standards along with an eclectic group of bookish Thais.

### 🍴 EAT ME *International* $$$$
☎ 0 2238 0931; 1/6 Soi Phiphat 2; 🕙 3pm-1am; 🚇 Sala Daeng, 🚆 Silom
Cosy yet cosmopolitan, Eat Me made Bangkok wake up and embrace the 21st century. It throws together smart fusion dishes, an eclectic wine list, cutting edge artwork and smooth modern design, coming up trumps night after night. Soi Phiphat 2 is located off Th Convent.

### 🍴 HARMONIQUE
*Thai-Chinese* $$
☎ 0 2630 6763; 22 Soi 34, Th Charoen Krung; 🕙 11am-10pm Mon-Sat ; 🚇 Tha Oriental; 🚻 🛗 Ⓥ

## ART CONQUISTADORS
Folks crow about Thailand's great gem buys, but all the deals have been cornered by scammers. For savvy shoppers with a stash of cash, check out the great Thai contemporary art buys. Asian art, especially from China and Vietnam, is all the rage with international buyers and speculators have their eye on Southeast Asia as the next art frontier. The city's galleries specialise in all manner of wall hangings from paint to prints and open new exhibits with social parties where Bangkok's cliques trade name cards and musings on Thailand. Check the English-language press for exhibition openings or visit the following galleries at quieter times: Thavibu Gallery (opposite), Gallery F-Stop (p125), H Gallery (p98) and Kathmandu Photo Gallery (p96).

If you have been burned by your courtship with Thai food, then let Harmonique whisper sweet nothings to your tender palate. Its reserved dishes are served in the courtyard of a rambling wooden house bubbling over with ambience, from the huge banyan tree draped with fairy lights to the marble-top tables.

### 🍴 INDIAN HUT *North Indian* $$$
☎ 0 2237 8812; 311/2-5 Th Surawong; 🕙 11am-11pm; 🚇 Tha Oriental; 🛗 Ⓥ
Paneer, paneer, paneer. We can't stress it enough: don't walk out the door of Indian Hut without

## THE MILLION BAHT MEAL

Recently Bangkok was shocked – not by the dissolution of democracy or by the proliferation of prostitution – but by a charity dinner that charged $1 million baht per plate. Everyone knows, said one vendor interviewed by the newspaper, that the best food in town only costs 30B a plate. He's right and any meal cheque that looks bigger than pocket change is usually charging for ambience, an element that is irrelevant to most Thai diners.

To décor or not: this is our dilemma. The average Bangkok tourist expects dinner to be an edible journey into the exoticism of Siam both in form and flavour. But for some reason, the two rarely meet harmoniously. There is a whole clique of restaurants in Bangkok specifically designed to impress visitors with their looks and little else. We won't name names but you'll soon meet and agree that Bangkok is best savoured if seated at a plastic table.

tasting its delectable homemade cottage cheese, preferably in its incarnation as part of the deceptively simple tomato and onion curry. Despite the fast-food overtones in the name of the restaurant, this place is very classy and popular with businesspeople.

### 🍴 KALPAPRUEK RESTAURANT
*Thai-Italian* $$
☎ 0 2236 4335; 27 Th Pramuan, Th Silom
The original branch of one of Bangkok's favourite Thai-*faràng* restaurants feeds extended families and discriminating couples. Also at the Emporium (p131).

### 🍴 KOZO SUSHI *Japanese* $$
☎ 0 2231 2202; 3rd fl, Thaniya Plaza, Soi Thaniya, Th Silom; 🕒 11.30am-2pm & 5.30-11pm; 🚇 Sala Daeng; 🚇 Silom; ♿ 🚻
If you need some purity in your diet, become a trainspotter along

the sushi tracks of this restaurant. But be prepared for some duelling chopsticks during the hugely popular all-you-can-eat lunch. Wait for the sushi chefs to restock the supply to get the freshest catch.

### 🍴 LE LYS *Thai* $$
☎ 0 2287 1898; 104 Soi 7, Th Narathiwat Ratchanakharin; 🕒 noon-10pm; 🚇 Chong Nonsi; ♿
More of a dinner party than a restaurant, Le Lys has uprooted its living/dining room to a new location and all their friends have followed. You'll still find all the pleasant Thai dishes, *pétanque* (French lawn bowling) in the backyard and the same gentle hospitality.

### 🍴 LE NORMANDIE *French* $$$$
☎ 0 2236 0400; Oriental Hotel, Soi Oriental, Th Charoen Krung; 🕒 noon-2.30pm & 7-10.30pm Mon-Sat; 🚇 Tha Oriental; ♿

Give yourself time to prepare for Le Normandie, one of Bangkok's finest. Make sure the jacket and tie are dry-cleaned and the booking is confirmed. Discipline your stomach and get your mind ready for some big decisions: the degustation or roast lobster with handmade egg noodles and bisque sauce? Leave room for the scrumptious raspberry gratin crowned with a raspberry liqueur ice cream.

## 🍴 MIZU'S KITCHEN
*Japanese* $$

☎ 0 2233 6447; 32 Soi Patpong 1, Th Silom; 🕙 11am-3am; 🚇 Sala Daeng, 🚇 Silom; 🚹 🚻

Warm and salty, Mizu's occupation-era fusion of Japanese and American dishes is really the perfect nightcap after a schedule of heavy drinking. Although your reflexes might be dulled, use the red-and-white chequered tablecloth to screen yourself from the soy sauce–hissing hot plates.

## 🍴 SARA-JANE'S *Isan-Italian* $$

☎ 0 2676 3338; 55/21 Narathiwat Ratchanakharin; 🕙 11am-9pm; 🚕 taxi; 🚹 🚻

A real circus at lunchtime, this restaurant (named after the American founder who married a Thai) knows how to make Isan food speak *faràng*. That's why expats keep coming back for *yam sôm*

*oh* (pomelo salad) and *kài yâang* (grilled chicken).

## 🍴 SOI PRADIT (SOI 20) MARKET *Thai* $

Soi 20, Th Silom; 🕙 10am-10pm; 🚌 504; 🚹 🚻

Bangkok's magic is working if you start craving spontaneous street-stall meals instead of air-conditioned luxury. During the day, fruit vendors and noodle shops line this narrow *soi* leading to Masjid Mirasuddeen mosque. Look for the duck noodle shop (identified by a, um, duck sign) or rickety tables selling zesty *khànǒm jiin* (stark white rice noodles served with curries). The woks are still sizzling at night

Grab pre-party bites and bevvies on Soi 4, Th Silom

## CRUISING FOR DINNER

Dinner cruises swim along the Mae Nam Chao Phraya at night, far away from the heat and noise of the city but basking in the twinkling lights. These floating buffets range from sophisticated to home style and several sail underneath Saphan Phra Ram IX, the longest single-span cable-suspension bridge in the world. The food of course runs a distant second to the ambience.

**Yok Yor Marina & Restaurant** ( ☎ 0 2863 0565; www.yokyor.co.th; 885 Soi Somdet Chao Phraya 17, Thonburi; adult/child 120/60B, à la carte menu, dishes start at 150B; ⏱ 8-10pm) is a favourite among Thais celebrating birthdays.

**Wan Fah Cruises** ( ☎ 0 2639 0704; River City shopping complex; dinner cruise 780-680B; ⏱ 7-9pm) is a buxom wooden boat with Thai music and traditional dance.

**Manohra Cruises** (Map pp140–1; ☎ 0 2476 0022; www.manohracruises.com; Bangkok Marriott Resort & Spa, Thonburi; dinner cruise adult 1700B, cocktail cruise 500B; ⏱ dinner cruise 7.30-10pm, cocktail cruise 6-7pm) commands a fleet of converted teak barges that part the waters with regal flair.

when more sit-down stalls start to appear.

### 🍴 SOMBOON SEAFOOD
*Chinese Seafood* $$$

☎ 0 2234 3104; 169/7-11 Th Surawong; ⏱ 4-11.30pm; 🚌 75, 93; & ♿ V

Holy seafood factory: ascending the many staircases to a free table might make you nervous about the quality of so much quantity. But Somboon's famous crab curry will make you messy and full. Dainty eaters can opt for the slightly more surgical pursuit of devouring a whole fried fish.

### 🍴 TALING PLING *Thai* $$
☎ 0 2234 4872; 60 Th Pan; 🚇 Chong Nonsi; ⏱ 11am-11pm

You know you've picked well when Thai families outnumber

expats. And you get a stylish setting, pretty enough for Bangkok gays. A few menu standouts include *yam plaa salid taling pling* (a fried fish salad with the namesake sour vegetable), chicken wrapped in pandanus leaves and *phàk dam lung* (stir-fried gourd leaves). Located off Th Silom.

### 🍴 TONGUE THAI *Thai* $$
☎ 0 2630 9918/9; 18-20 Soi 38, Th Charoen Krung; ⏱ 11am-11pm; ⚓ Tha Oriental; & V

Maybe the name is supposed to remind us of the chef's honourable intentions to not sacrifice Thai flavours to Western palates. Whatever the case, your tongue will be feeling most Thai as it wraps itself around the flavoursome morsels of Tongue Thai's spicy eggplant salad.

# 🍸 DRINK

The *soi* around Patpong undergo various surges in popularity as a drinking-and-clubbing scene. Even if things are in a slump, you'll still need to wet your whistle after bargaining at the Patpong Night Market. See Play for club recommendations.

## 🍸 BALCONY BAR *Gay & Lesbian*
☎ 0 2235 5891; www.balconypub.com; 8/6-8 Soi 4, Th Silom; ⏱ 5pm-2am; 🚇 Sala Daeng, Ⓜ Silom; ♿
Balcony is your classic all-round, good-time bar, where hot pants and string vests check out the talent and tables of straight couples order countless rounds. A table outside under the red lanterns is the prime position for watching the passing parade.

## 🍸 BAMBOO BAR *Live Music*
☎ 0 2659 9000; Oriental Hotel, 48 Soi Oriental, Th Charoen Krung; ⏱ 11am-2am Fri & Sat, 11am-1am Sun-Thu; 🚇 Saphan Taksin; ♿
You could be forgiven for thinking that Thailand was a British colony when you visit the Bamboo Bar, the city's top jazz spot. Patrons sip G&Ts while lounging in leopard-print chairs, feeling a million miles away from the heat and dust, while jazz bands or singers soothe any remaining tensions.

## 🍸 O'REILLY'S *Bar*
☎ 0 2632 7515; 62/1-2 Th Silom, cnr Soi Thaniya; ⏱ 11am-1am; 🚇 Sala Daeng, Ⓜ Lumphini
A squeaky clean facsimile of an Irish pub, O'Reilly's earns its shamrock for its affordable happy hour specials. Its location, central to the nightspots scattered around Patpong and Silom, also makes it a meeting spot for far-flung friends.

## 🍸 SIROCCO & SKY BAR *Bar*
☎ 0 2624 9555; The Dome, 1055 Th Silom; ⏱ 6pm-1am
Descend the sweeping stairs like a Hollywood diva to the precipice bar of this rooftop restaurant. A dress code is enforced and drink prices are impressive, but so is the view.

## IN THE KNOW
Need to know the hottest new restaurant or the latest chic bar? Bangkok morphs more quickly than the print before you, so to keep up check out *Bangkok 101*, a stylish monthly magazine following new openings and happenings. Or pick up *BKK Magazine*, available free at bars and restaurants and aimed at a younger set. Bangkok Recorder (www.bangkokrecorder.com) watches the DJ scene and Bangkok Gig Guide (www.bangkokgigguide.com) catalogues live music showings.

## ☂ TAPAS *Bar*

☎ 0 2632 7883; www.tapasroom.net;
114/7 Soi 4, Th Silom; 🕒 10pm-2am;
🚇 Sala Daeng, Ⓜ Lumphini; ♿

When patrons first arrive, this
Moorish-style bar is mellow, with
wavering candlelight. Everyone lies
back against big cushions, nodding
to the chilled-out house beats.
Later the disco ball starts swirling
and the dance floor gets sweaty.

## ☂ TELEPHONE *Gay & Lesbian*

☎ 0 2234 3279; www.telephonepub
.com; 114/11-13 Soi 4, Th Silom; 🕒 5pm-
1am; 🚇 Sala Daeng, Ⓜ Silom; ♿

Muscle boys and queens parade
past the outdoor tables at Telephone, one of Bangkok's oldest,
most popular gay bars. Inside, each
table has a telephone you can use
to call any patrons you fancy.

## ☂ THREE SIXTY *Bar*

☎ 0 2442 2000; 32nd fl, Millennium
Hilton, 123 Th Charoen Nakorn, Thonburi;
🕒 5pm-1pm; 🚢 shuttle boat from Tha
Sathon

Even if you no longer have to count
pennies, this hotel champagne bar
tastes much better when someone
else is picking up the tab. Then
you can let the bubbles tickle your
throat as you soak in the view of
Bangkok from across the river.

## ☂ V9 *Bar*

☎ 0 2238 1991; 37th fl, Sofitel, Th Silom;
🕒 5pm-2am; 🚇 Chong Nonsi

The décor would even make
Liberace cringe but this top-floor
wine bar wins fans for its afford-
ably priced bottles of wine and
its safe-from-the-rain view of
Bangkok.

Meeker now, but the red lights still flicker in infamous Patpong

# ⭐ PLAY

Despite being home to Patpong's 'ping-pong' strip clubs, you can collect holiday moments that don't need censoring. Try out a Thai cooking class or massage therapy (the legitimate version).

## 🔲 BLUE ELEPHANT COOKING SCHOOL *Cooking School*

☎ 0 2673 9353; www.blueelephant .com; 233 Th Sathon Tai; classes 2800B; ☷ 8.30am-12.30pm & 1-5pm; 🚇 Surasak

Devotees of Julia Child will enjoy the culinary professionalism of this restaurant-associated school. Both sessions get a main course of Thai cooking theory and hands-on meal preparation of four courses. Morning classes include a market tour.

## 🔲 DJ STATION *Gay & Lesbian*

☎ 0 2266 4029; 8/6-8 Soi 2, Th Silom; ☷ 10pm-2am; 🚇 Sala Daeng, 🚇 Silom

Neo-industrial DJ Station is a long-standing dance club in a town that loves change. The music varies wildly from handbag to hard house but the dance floor remains packed with shirtless sweaty boys. If you don't like the scene here, this tiny *soi* has an avenue's worth of options so move along and take your pick.

## 🔲 EPICUREAN KITCHEN *Cooking School*

☎ 0 2631 1119; www.thaikitchen.com; sub-soi off 10/2 Soi Convent, Th Silom; classes 2000B; ☷ 9.30am-12.30pm Mon-Fri; 🚇 Sala Daeng, 🚇 Silom

Sponsored by the Thai Kitchen brand, Epicurean Kitchen offers a rotating menu, individual cooking stations and a less formal approach than the hotel cooking schools. Your barbecues will thank you for studying on Tuesday, which includes spicy chilli sauces from the northeast region of Thailand.

## 🔲 FORTUNE TELLERS *Fortune Tellers*

☎ 0 2234 8060; mezzanine level, Montien Hotel, Th Surawong; 550B; ☷ 10am-4pm; 🚇 Sala Daeng, 🚇 Silom; 🚻

Thais regard fortune tellers as professional consultants whose guidance is sought for picking auspicious dates to start

## STRAIGHT TO THE MOON

You have to be high to think that Bangkok is beautiful. High in altitude, that is. Locals love to show off their overgrown town from the rooftop bars that pair tummy butterflies with cocktails. Toast the town from these rooftop bars (smart casual dress): Sirocco & Sky Bar (p107), V9 (opposite), Moon Bar at Vertigo (p116) and Three Sixty (opposite).

businesses or marriages. In the most Thai of Thai hotels, space is devoted to this important business service, which includes two English speakers (a palmist and tarot-card reader).

### ▣ FREEMAN *Gay & Lesbian*
☎ 0 2632 8032; sub-soi btwn Soi 2 & Soi Thaniya, Th Silom; ⏱ 11.30pm-1am; ☒ Sala Daeng, ☉ Silom

Reputedly the best lady-boy cabaret in town. The midnight shows are a little raunchier than the typical tourist-oriented shows of Broadway homage and pink taffeta.

### ▣ HEALTHLAND SPA & MASSAGE *Spa*
☎ 0 2263 7883; www.healthlandspa .com; cnr Soi 12 & Th Sathon Neua; ⏱ 9am-11pm; ☒ Surasak; ♿

The name and the super-sized setting might suggest massage factory, but Bangkok locals swear this is one of the best value massages in the city. The massage component of this business started out as an add-on service to an organic grocery store in the Bangkok suburbs.

### ▣ LUCIFER *Dance Club*
☎ 0 2234 6902; www.luciferdisko.com; Soi Patpong 1, Th Silom; ⏱ 8pm-2am; ☒ Sala Daeng, ☉ Lumphini

This is no burn-baby-burn disco inferno. Sure, there's a cute papier-

mâché devil at the entrance, but Lucifer is a serious club for hardcore techno. Good old Lucifer is also affordable enough to be a hell of a good time almost every night. You'll find it on the second floor above Radio City.

### ▣ ORIENTAL HOTEL COOKING CENTRE *Cooking School*
☎ 0 2659 9000; www.mandarinoriental .com; 48 Th Oriental; classes US$120; ⏱ 9am-noon; ⛴ free shuttle boat from Oriental Hotel

With an intimate setting, you might well forget that you're in the old world of the Oriental Hotel. Daily classes begin with a lecture, which is followed by individual preparation. Considering the price, opt for the daily menu that contains more complex dishes, such as *hàw mòk* (fish curry mousse), rather than a basic *phàt thai*.

## ⭐ ORIENTAL SPA THAI HEALTH & BEAUTY CENTRE *Spa*

☎ 0 2439 7613; www.mandarinoriental .com; Oriental Hotel, 48 Soi Oriental, Th Charoen Krung; day packages from US$100; ⏰ 9am-10pm; 🚤 free shuttle from Oriental Hotel; ♿

One of the cities most private and intimate spas, the Oriental has only 14 rooms in a classic setting. You won't find a lot of bells and whistles here, just the necessary niceties. The most popular therapy on offer is the jet lag massage, which will help reset an obstinate body clock.

## ⭐ RUEN-NUAD MASSAGE *Massage*

☎ 0 2632 2662; 42 Th Convent, Th Silom; ⏰ 10am-10pm; 🚇 Sala Daeng Ⓜ Silom

For a Goldilocks massage (not too hard, not too soft), Ruen-Nuad offers a tranquil spa-like setting but at parlour shop prices.

## ⭐ SALA RIM NAAM *Theatre*

☎ 0 2437 3080; Oriental Hotel, 48 Soi Oriental, Th Charoen Krung; 1850/1450B ⏰ 7-10pm; 🚤 free shuttle boat from Oriental Hotel; ♿ 🚻

Riverside Sala Rim Naam, a stunning Thai pavilion made of teak, marble and bronze, holds nightly classical dance performances preceded by a set Thai meal. Part of the Oriental Hotel cultural programme.

## ⭐ SILOM THAI COOKING SCHOOL *Cooking School*

☎ 0 4726 5669; 31/11 Soi 13, Th Silom; classes 1000B; ⏰ 9.30am-noon; 🚇 Chong Nonsi; ♿

Run out of a private home, this is both an introduction to home-cooking and ordinary Thai life. The setting is rustic (and not hyper hygienic) and you chop shallots while sitting cross-legged on the floor, pound chillies into paste, and fry it all up in the pan. Includes a market tour and five dishes.

### WORTH THE TRIP

Looking for a day at the races? Horseracing is alive and well in the kingdom and brings out the same frenzied energy of gambling and drinking as it does elsewhere. The public seats are right beside the finish line and horses kick up mud and sweat as they thunder past. There are English-language schedules and unhelpful betting tips handed out by every bystander. The races are held every Sunday, either at the **Royal Bangkok Sports Club** (Map p81, C3; ☎ 0 2251 018186; 1 Th Henri Dunant; 🚇 Ratchadamri), which hosts two Sundays a month, or the **Royal Turf Club** (Map p140–1, B5; ☎ 0 2628 1810; 183 Th Phitsanulok; 🚌 509), which hosts the alternate Sundays. The Royal Turf Club also hosts Bangkok's biggest horse race, the King's Cup, around the first or second week of January.

# >LUMPHINI

Just when Bangkok seemed hopelessly congested, foresighted city officials preserved Lumphini Park as the city's central green space in the 1920s. The tropical heat shoos away visitors during the day but the cooler temperatures of the morning and evening bring out Bangkokians' sporty side.

The area surrounding the park is prime real estate for foreign embassies on the divided roadway of Th Sathon. Closer to the park is a resuscitated nightspot of itsy bitsy clubs on Th Sarasin. Th Phra Ram IV is one of the city's bulkiest thoroughfares with a traffic flyover that provides one of the best views of the city from a car window. Branching off Th Phra Ram IV is the ageing backpacker scene around Soi Ngam Duphli. The Lumphini subway station has made it easier to get in and out of the area, which is otherwise strangled by uncrossable intersections and relentless traffic.

## LUMPHINI

### ⊙ SEE
Lumphini Park ............... 1  B2

### 🛍 SHOP
Suan Lum Night
Bazaar ............................ 2  C3

### 🍴 EAT
Baan Khanitha &
Gallery ........................... 3  A4

Cyan ................................ 4  B4
D'Sens ............................ 5  A3
Soi Polo Fried Chicken .... 6  D2

### 🍸 DRINK
Moon Bar at Vertigo .. (see 10)
Vino di Zanotti ............... 7  B3
Wong's Place ................. 8  D5

### ★ PLAY
70's Bar & I-Chub ........... 9  B1
Banyan Tree Spa ........... 10  B4
Brown Sugar ................. 11  B1
Joe Louis Puppet
Theatre ......................... 12  C3
Lumphini Boxing
Stadium ........................ 13  C3
Met Bar ...................... (see 4)
Shela ............................ 14  B1
Sukhothai Hotel ........... 15  B4

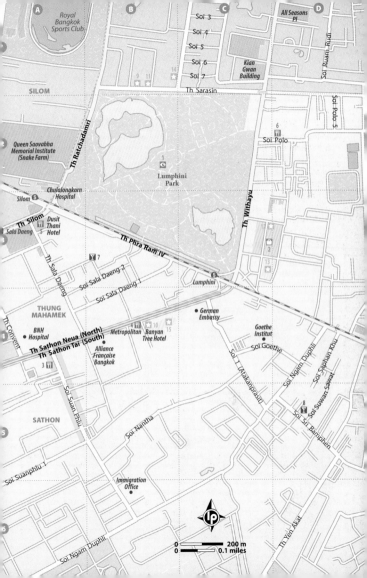

A

Royal
Bangkok
Sports Club

B

C

Soi 3
Soi 4
Soi 5
Soi 6
Soi 7

D

All Seasons
Pl

Soi Ruam Rudi

SILOM

9 11

14

Th Sarasin

Kian
Gwan
Building

Soi Polo 5

Queen Saovabha
Memorial Institute
(Snake Farm)

Th Ratchadamri

1

Lumphini
Park

6

Soi Polo

Chulalongkorn
Hospital

Silom S

Th Silom

Sala Daeng S

Dusit
Thani
Hotel

Th Sala Daeng

Th Phra Ram IV

Th Withayu

2

13

7

Soi Sala Daeng 2

Soi Sala Daeng 1

Lumphini S

Lumphini

THUNG
MAHAMEK

BNH
Hospital

Th Sathon Neua (North)
Th Sathon Tai (South)

Th Convent

Metropolitan

10
Banyan
Tree Hotel

15

German
Embassy

Goethe
Institut

Soi Goethe

Alliance
Française
Bangkok

3

Soi Ngam Duphii

Soi 1 (Itakanpradit)

Soi Saphan Khu

Soi Suan Plu

SATHON

Soi Nantha

8

Soi Suwan-Sawat

Soi Sri Bamphen

Soi Suanphlu 1

Immigration
Office

Th Yen Akat

Soi Ngam Duphii

0          200 m
0          0.1 miles

##  SEE

### LUMPHINI PARK

**Th Phra Ram IV; admission free;** 5am-8pm; Sala Daeng, Lumphini or Silom; 507, 76;

Bangkok's biggest central park, located between Th Withayu and Th Ratchadamri, has nurtured many a bike rider, jogger, *tàkrâw* (a Thai football game) player and t'ai chi practitioner. After developing the Bangkok cough, try a few gulps of fresh air at Lumphini. For more information see p28.

##  SHOP

### SUAN LUM NIGHT BAZAAR
*Market*

**cnr Th Withayu & Th Phra Ram IV;** Lumphini

Only a few years old, this nighttime souvenir market, across from the park, was just finding its niche when developers announced its closure. Possible redevelopment includes Thailand's tallest skyscraper, yet another megamall and maybe even a faux floating market. But court battles

And if daytime markets aren't enough, Suan Lum Night Bazaar fulfils all twilight shopping needs

## STREET FOOD

Eating like a Thai means grabbing a plastic chair beside a little vendor cart or an outdoor market. Below are a few street-food recommendations and tips on spotting their purveyors. The book *Thai Hawker Food* (available at most Bangkok bookstores) is also a good start for getting your bearings for street food.

> *sôm-tam* (green papaya salad) – look for a large wooden mortar and order it with *khâo nĭaw* (sticky rice).
> *phàt thai* (thin rice noodles with tofu, vegetables, egg and peanuts) – any vendor with a wok can make this, but quality varies.
> *kŭaytǐaw phàt khîi mao* (literally 'shit-drunk noodles'; wide rice noodles combined with meat, vegetables, chilli and Thai basil) – another wok wonder.
> *khâo phàt* (stir-fried rice) – also available from wok vendors.
> *khâo man kài* (chicken and rice) – look for carcasses of boiled chicken in the display case.

between competing interests have kept the night bazaar in limbo and the rest of us guessing about the site's future. Although there are still some vendors, no one knows how long they'll remain before being evicted. Have a look for yourself, if you're in the neighbourhood.

 ## EAT

 **BAAN KHANITHA & GALLERY** *Thai*   $$$
☎ 0 2253 4638/9; 69 Th Sathon Tai; ⏲ 11am-2pm & 6-11pm; ◉ Lumphini
Baan Khanitha is one of Bangkok's classic expat restaurants. Why? It's got the formula down pat: outstanding food, high-class setting and impeccable service. There's also an art gallery onsite.

**CYAN** *International*   $$$$
☎ 0 2625 3333; Metropolitan Hotel, 27 Th Sathon Tai; ⏲ 6am-10.30am, noon-2pm & 6.30pm-10.30pm; ⓡ Sala Daeng, ◉ Lumphini
Fresh and intense flavours inspired by the Mediterranean give substance to this minimalist fashion spot. Executive chef Amanda Gale, a protégée of Australian celebrity chef Neil Perry, uses seasonal and zesty ingredients to rouse eaters out of their tropical stupor.

**D'SENS** *French*   $$$$
☎ 0 2200 9000; 22nd fl, Dusit Thani, 946 Th Phra Ram IV; ⏲ noon-3pm & 6-11pm; ⓡ Sala Daeng, ◉ Silom
Atop the Dusit Thani, overlooking Lumphini Park, this is the latest venture for the wonder-twins Laurent and Jacques Pourcel,

## EAT YOUR HEART OUT

An eating contest with class? Indeed, the decadent hotel buffets push moderate eaters into overdrive as they make several laps through the stations loaded with seafood, braised meats, sashimi, raw oysters and a chocolate fountain. Most brunches are on Sunday from 11.30am–3pm; call for details and advance reservations.

**Royal Orchid Sheraton** (Map p95, B2; ☎ 0 2266 0123; Soi Captain Bush/Soi 30, Th Charoen Krung; 750B) has a scenic riverside setting and enough kid's activities to feed families with food and fun.

**Four Seasons Hotel** (Map p81, C3; ☎ 0 2250 1000; Th Ratchadamri; 2150B) generously fills a foie gras counter, free-flowing champagne and a decadent price tag.

**Sukhothai Hotel** ( ☎ 0 2344 8888; 13 Th Sathon Tai; 1600B) hosts a weekend brunch with free-flowing wines (300B extra) and all the fixings.

creators of the Michelin-starred Le Jardin des Sens in Montpellier France. The restaurant is handsome yet modern and the menu draws from the traditions of the south of France, relying mainly on high-quality French imports for its ingredients.

### 🍴 SOI POLO FRIED CHICKEN
*Thai* $$

☎ 0 2655 8489; 137/1-2 Soi Polo, Th Withayu; ⏱ 7am-7pm; 🚇 Ploenchit; 🚻 🚼

Your nose will lead you to what many claim is the best *kài thâwt* (fried chicken) in town; it certainly bitch-slaps KFC. It's golden and crispy on the outside with lots of fried garlic bits. One half-order will generously feed two. In order to eat like a local, order sticky rice and employ the spicy dipping sauces.

# 🍸 DRINK

### 🍸 MOON BAR AT VERTIGO
*Bar*

☎ 0 2679 1200; Banyan Tree Hotel, 21/100 Th Sathon Tai

This sky-high, open-air bar will literally take your breath away. The elevator delivers you to the 59th floor of the Banyan Tree Hotel where you weave your way through dimly lit hallways to the roar of Bangkok traffic far below. Come at sunset and gravitate to the right of the bar for more impressive views.

### 🍸 VINO DI ZANOTTI *Bar*

☎ 0 2636 3366; 41 Soi Yommarat, Th Silom; ⏱ 6pm-midnight; 🚇 Sala Daeng 🚇 Lumphini

Classy and mature, this wine bar is a well-mannered date. The jazz band is never deafening, the

There's such a thing as too much choice – Lumphini's food stalls are living proof

arctic air-con ventilates the cigarette smoke and the wines can be paired with victuals from the affiliated Italian trattoria to keep the spirits from having their way with you. It's off Soi Sala Daeng.

 **WONG'S PLACE** *Bar*
**27/3 Soi Sri Bamphen, Th Phra Ram I;**
🚇 **Lumphini**
A relic from the backpacker world of the early 1980s, Wong's Place (off Soi Ngam Duphli) is a homey after-hours drinking spot with an old-school soundtrack. Good for bleary-eyed tale-spinning.

## ⭐ PLAY
The gay bars on Th Sarasin make up one angle of Bangkok's gay triangle, connecting the bars and clubs on Soi 2 and Soi 4, Th Silom (see the Drink, p107, and Play, p109, sections).

⭐ **BANYAN TREE SPA** *Spa*
☎ **0 2679 1052; www.banyantree.com;**
**21st fl, Banyan Tree, 21/100 Th Sathon Tai; day packages from US$90;** 🕐 **9am–10pm;** 🚊 **Sala Daeng,** 🚇 **Lumphini;** ♿
Way up high, almost in the heavens, this 21st-floor spa is one

Hangin' buff at Lumphini Park (p114)

of the most luxurious in the city. Decked out in new millennium tranquillity, the spa uses deep-tissue massages, body wraps in warming spices and a flower bath finale to transport your further into the beyond.

### ⭐ BROWN SUGAR *Live Music*
☎ 0 2250 1825; 231/20 Th Sarasin; ☙ 5pm-1am; 🚇 Chitlom
Evoking the intimacy of New Orleans jazz clubs, this compact bar lends an ear to be-bop and ragtime, leaving the smooth sounds to the hotel lobbies. On Sunday nights, the high-powered musicians who are touring the

luxury hotels assemble here for impromptu jam sessions.

### ⭐ JOE LOUIS PUPPET THEATRE *Theatre*
☎ 0 2252 9683; www.joelouis-theater .com; Suan Lum Night Bazaar, cnr Th Phra Ram IV & Th Withayu; admission 900B; ☙ show 7.30pm; 🚇 Lumphini; 🚻 🚹
The ancient art of Thai puppetry (*lákhon lék*) was rescued by the late Sakorn Yangkhiawsod, more popularly known as Joe Louis, in 1985. Today Joe's children carry on the tradition, presenting elaborate performances of *Ramakian* and Thai myths.

### ⭐ LUMPHINI BOXING STADIUM *Muay Thai*
☎ 0 2251 4303; Th Phra Ram IV; 🚇 Lumphini
The big-time *muay thai* fighters spar at Lumphini's coveted ring.

### FEEDING THE SPIRITS
The small houses that sit in front of private homes and businesses aren't for child's play but for paranormal comfort. Known as spirit houses, these structures are intended for a site's guardian spirit. Daily offerings of joss sticks, flower garlands, fruit (oranges or coconuts) or a set of three small bowls (containing rice, sweetmeats and water) are set out to keep the spirit sated and to ensure the flow of good fortune.

## HIGH KICKS

The most dynamic and exciting Thai sport is *muay thai*, orThai boxing, considered by many to be the ultimate in hand-to-hand fighting. Matches can be violent, but the surrounding spectacle of crazy music, pre-match rituals and manic betting is half the draw. When a Thai boxer is ready for the ring, he is given a fighting name – usually a none-too-subtle reminder of how much pain these guys aim to inflict. Just so you know what you might be in for, recent clashes pitted such fighters as Dangerous Uneven-Legged Man vs the Bloody Elbow; the Human Stone vs the King of the Knee; and No Mercy Killer vs the Golden Left Leg. Fights are held at Ratchadamnoen Boxing Stadium (p65) and at Lumphini Boxing Stadium (opposite).

Matches occur on Tuesday, Friday and Saturday at 6pm. Tickets cost 1000/1500/2000B (3rd class/2nd class/ringside). The stadium doesn't usually fill up until the main event around 8pm. For the past two years, there has been talk of the Lumphini Stadium moving to a new location on Th Nang Linji but, at the time of research, a final decision had not reached a conclusion. You'll find the stadium near the intersection of Th Withayu.

### MET BAR *Dance Club*
☎ 0 2625 3333; Metropolitan Hotel, Th Sathon; 6pm-2am; Lumphini
Cosy and fashionable, the Met Bar started its career as a members-only club but has since relaxed its policy to include everyone dressed to impress. The Friday night theme nights get the most attention, but in fickle Bangkok the Met's social standing is not guaranteed.

### TH SARASIN GAY CLUBS
*Gay & Lesbian*
Th Sarasin; 6pm-1am; Ratchadamri
This quiet little street across from Lumphini Park has a tight cluster of intimate bars, ranging from non-orientational to gay-festive. There's disco fever at 70s Bar (☎ 0 2253 4433) and karaoke at I-Chub (☎ 0 2650 5598), a bar dedicated to bears and their admirers. Bangkok has just started to develop a lesbian-only nightclub scene with two newcomers: Shela (Soi Lang Suan, Th Ploenchit) and Zeta (p148). You'll find the clubs located between Th Ratchadamri and Soi Lang Suan.

# >SUKHUMVIT

The most urban and cosmopolitan part of Bangkok, Th Sukhumvit arches from the alleged centre of the city all the way to the Gulf of Thailand. Along the lower-numbered *soi*, the street is home to a thriving sex-tourism scene (namely Nana Entertainment Plaza and Soi Cowboy), while the city's elite live and play at the more respectable upper end. Every version of accomplished expat – from formerly exiled aristocratic Thais to Japanese executives – claims a Sukhumvit address and the commercial corridor caters to these big budget tastes.

## SUKHUMVIT

### ◉ SEE
Ban Kamthieng & Siam
Society..........................1 C3
Benjasiri Park .................2 D4
Chuvit Garden ................3 B2
Play Gallery .............. (see 12)
Thailand Creative &
Design Center.............. (see 6)

### 🏠 SHOP
Almeta..........................4 C2
Asia Books ...................5 B2
Asia Books ................(see 6)
Emporium .....................6 D4
Gallery F-Stop .......... (see 30)
Greyhound .................(see 6)
Jaspal .......................(see 6)
Jim Thompson ...........(see 6)
Kinokuniya ...................7 D4
L' Arcadia.....................8 C3
Nandakwang...................9 D2
Nickermann's Tailors....10 A2
Phu Fa........................11 B2
Playground!.................12 H2
Propaganda.................(see 6)
Raja's Fashions ............13 A2
Rasi Sayam ..................14 D3

### 🍴 EAT
Ana's Garden ...............15 G5
Atlanta Coffee Shop.....16 A3
Baanya.........................17 B1
Bed Supperclub............18 B1
→ Cabbages & Condoms ..19 B3
→ Crepes & Co .................20 B3
Dosa King ....................21 C2
Federal Hotel Coffee
Shop ...........................22 B1
Giusto .........................23 C2
Greyhound Café ..........(see 6)
Horng Ahaan ...............24 G5
Kalpapruek on First.....(see 6)
Kuppa .........................25 C4
Nasir al-Masri...............26 A1
Pizzeria Bella Napoli ...27 D3
Ruen-Mallika................28 C5
Soi 38 Night Market .....29 G6
→ Tamarind Café ............30 D4
Vientiane Kitchen ........31 F5

### 🍸 DRINK
Cheap Charlie's.............32 B2
Koi ..............................33 C4
Sin Bar ........................34 A2

### ⭐ PLAY
Baan Thai Wellness
Retreat .......................35 E5
Bed Supperclub......... (see 18)
Buathip Thai
Massage ......................36 B1
DVN Spa & Wellbeing
Centre..........................37 D4
First Ave Beauty Salon..38 A1
Living Room .................39 C3
Q Bar...........................40 B1
Rasayana Retreat..........41 E3
SFX Cinema..................(see 6)
Salon de Bkk................(see 6)
World Fellowship of
Buddhists ..................(see 2)

Please see over for map

The money-hungry pursuits of shopping, bar-hopping and fashionable dining will occupy a Sukhumvit outing. A more down-home activity is a visit to Bangkok's Little Arabia, crammed into Soi 3/1. Hummus not curry dominates the restaurant menus and most customers stop in to bubble the water pipes and catch-up on Al Jazeera.

Although Sukhumvit is an endless traffic jam, the Skytrain makes plenty of far-flung spots more accessible.

 # SEE

## ◖ BAN KAMTHIENG

☎ 0 2661 6470; Siam Society, 131 Soi 21/Soi Asoke, Th Sukhumvit; 100/50B; ☾ 9am-5pm Mon-Sat; 🚇 Asoke, Ⓜ Sukhumvit

Ban Kamthieng is an excellent merging of pretty architecture with museum learning. Built in the Lanna style, this 1844 house shows how a northern Thai family lived, complete with thorough explanations of Lanna beliefs, rituals and ceremonies. This is one of Bangkok's best house museums with well-signed displays, video installations and clear descriptions of rituals. Plus you never have to share space with others.

## ◖ BENJASIRI PARK

btwn Soi 22 & Soi 24, Th Sukhumvit; ☾ 5am-8pm; admission free; 🚇 Phrom Phong; ♿

In summer, this park, built to honour Queen Sirikit's 60th birthday, hosts many open-air events. Set around an ornamental lake, most of the surrounding lawn space is taken by canoodling couples and teenage mating rituals-in-progress. If you're lucky you might spy a game of *tàkrâw* (a Thai foot game played with a rattan ball).

## ◖ CHUVIT GARDEN

Th Sukhumvit; admission free; ☾ 6am-7pm; 🚇 Nana; ♿

The story behind this park is shadier than the plantings. Khun Chuvit, the benefactor of the park, was Bangkok's biggest massage parlour owner. He was arrested in 2003 for illegally bulldozing, rather than legally evicting, tenants off the land where the park now stands (between Soi 8 and 10). With all the media attention, he sang like a bird about the police bribes he handed out during his career and became an unlikely activist against police corruption. Chuvit later ran unsuccessfully for Bangkok governor in 2004 and successfully for the Thai parliament in 2005. This park was one of his campaign promises. It's a pretty green patch in a neighbourhood lean on trees.

**Grid references (left margin):** 1 2 3 4 5 6

**Column references (top):** A B C D

Bumrungrad Hospital

Soi 1 (Soi Lang Suan)
Soi 3 (Soi Nana Nua)
Soi 3/1
Soi 5
Soi 9
Soi 7

Ploenchit

40
26
18
22
17
36
32

JW Marriott Bangkok
10
13

Nana Entertainment Plaza
11

34

Nana

Th Sukhumvit
Soi 2 (Soi Phasak)
Soi 4 (Nana Tai)

Th Sukhumvit Market

Chuvit Garden

Atlanta Hotel
16

Soi 6
Soi 8
Soi 10
Soi 12

Swiss Park Hotel
Soi 13
Soi 15

Ruamchit Plaza
5

Westin Grande Sukhumvit
Soi 19
Soi 11

Sheraton Grande Sukhumvit
39
19
20
21

Asoke
Sukhumvit

Soi 17
Tourist Police

TH SUKHUMVIT
Soi 23 (Prasanmit)

Soi 21 (Asok)
4
23
8
9
14

Soi 25
Soi 27
Soi 29 (Lat Khet)
Soi 31 (Sawasdee)
Soi 33 (Daeng Udom)
Soi Prasanmit

Rang Mahal
33
Soi 22
27

Benjasiri Park
2

Th Ratchadaphisek

Benjakiti Park

Soi 16
Soi 18
30
25
28

KHLONG TOEY

Chalerm Mahanakhon Expwy

Port-Din Daeng Expwy
Soi Phukchit

Sirikit Centre

Queen Sirikit Convention Centre

Khlong Toey

Th Phra Ram IV

Soi 24

Talat Khlong Toey

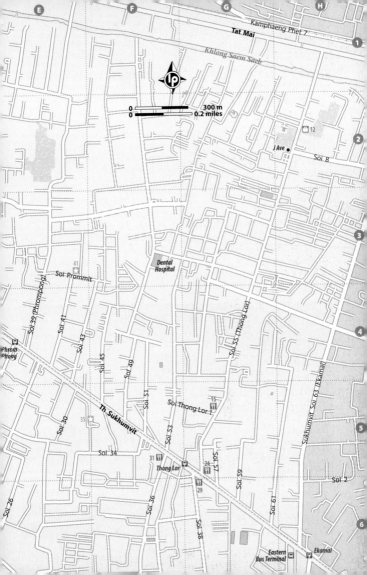

### ☺ PLAY GALLERY

☎ 0 2714 7888; www.playgroundstore
.co.th; Playground!, 2nd fl, 818 Soi 55, Th
Sukhumvit; 🕙 10am-11pm; 🚇 Thong
Lor, then red soi bus

The top-floor of this concept mall
spotlights offbeat art, from graffiti
to performance and a few genres
in between.

### ☺ THAILAND CREATIVE & DESIGN CENTER

☎ 0 2664 8448; www.tcdc.or.th; 6th
fl, Emporium, Th Sukhumvit; admission
free; 🕙 10.30am-10pm Tue-Sun;
🚇 Phrom Phong; ♿

An edu-tainment museum and
resource centre, the TCDC spotlights modern design from famous
fashion houses to image-brand-
ing products. Past exhibits have
included a history of the Finnish
company Marimekko as well as a
retrospective of cool gadgets. The
intention of the centre is to foster
and inspire Thailand's fledgling
industry of industrial design.

## 🛍 SHOP

Looking for a reputable tailor or
high-end fashion? Well, you've
come to the right neighbourhood.
If you need more pedestrian items
you're also in the right place –
Th Sukhumvit's souvenir market
stretches from Soi 2 to Soi 12 and

No end of beautiful bits in the Emporium's specialty shops

## SUIT YOURSELF

It is possible to get a tailor-made suit in Bangkok that will wear well in New York and London, but don't jump into the changing room with just any needle pusher. Finding a good tailor is an involved courtship that requires sartorial savvy. Also be aware that Bangkok's tailors are a conservative lot, more adept at the pinstripe banker look than skin-tight playboy.
> First, check out the suit racks back home to determine quality and costs.
> Commission a few small items (shirts, pants) before returning for a high-priced suit.
> For a suit that will last a lifetime, pick a quality imported fabric from a tailor you trust.
> Insist on at least two fittings and be firm when asking for modifications; even the best tailors will send you home if you don't speak up about imperfections.

Soi 3 to Soi 15 every day except Monday.

### 🏠 ALMETA Fashion
☎ 0 2204 1413; www.almeta.com; 20/3 Soi 23, Th Sukhumvit; ⏰ 11am-7pm; 🚇 Asoke; ♿
If the verdant colours of Thai silk evoke frumpy society matrons, then you're a candidate for Almeta's toned-down earth-tones similar in hue to raw sugar or lotus blossoms.

### 🏠 ASIA BOOKS Books
☎ 0 2664 8545; Emporium, btwn Soi 22 & Soi 24, Th Sukhumvit; ⏰ 10am-9.30pm; 🚇 Phrom Phong
Bangkok's homegrown English-language bookstore has a slot amid the name brands of Sukhumvit's Emporium shopping centre. Asia Books also has branches in Siam Paragon (p83) and Siam Discovery Center (p88) shopping centres.

### 🏠 EMPORIUM Shopping Centre
☎ 0 2664 7100 btwn Soi 22 & Soi 24, Th Sukhumvit; ⏰ 10.30am-10pm Mon-Fri, 10am-10pm Sat & Sun; 🚇 Phrom Phong; ♿
This top-flight mall cleverly woos young urban princesses and matronly aristocrats by stocking the hippest of fashion designers (Miu Miu, Prada), hardcore luxury brands (Chanel, Rolex) and classy eateries (Greyhound Café, Salon de l'Oriental). Despite the catwalk sauntering of these high-society bag girls, it all comes together without a stitch of intimidation.

### 🏠 GALLERY F-STOP Gallery
☎ 0 2663 7421; www.galleryfstop.com; 27 Soi 20, Th Sukhumvit; ⏰ 3pm-midnight Mon-Fri, 10am-midnight Sat-Sun; 🚇 Asoke; ♿
Many Bangkok restaurants added art work to the dinner menu in an effort to rescue art from the 'dead zones' (traditional museums).

Gallery F-Stop (hosted by Tamarind Café, p133) stands apart as the city's only restaurant-gallery for photography.

### 📷 GREYHOUND *Fashion*
☎ 0 2260 7121; www.greyhound .co.th; 2nd fl, Emporium, Th Sukhumvit; 🕙 10.30am-10pm; 🚇 Phrom Phong; ♿
Greyhound makes sleek streetwear – basics with an edge – for urbanites. Like many fashion houses, it has expanded to become a lifestyle brand that includes minimalist cafés (see p131) and spin-off brands (Playhound and Grey). Also in Siam Center (p88) and Siam Paragon (p89) shopping centres.

### 📷 JASPAL *Fashion*
Emporium, btwn Soi 22 & Soi 24, Th Sukhumvit; 🕙 10.30am-9pm; 🚇 Phrom Phong
Snag some cute basics from this homegrown alternative to the Gap. Also at Siam Center (p84).

### 📷 JIM THOMPSON *Fashion*
Emporium, btwn Soi 22 & Soi 24, Th Sukhumvit; 🕙 10.30am-10pm; Skytrain Phrom Phong
Another outlet of the Thai silk company that carries more contemporary fashions. Also at Siam Paragon (p84) and on Th Surawong (p99).

### 📷 KINOKUNIYA BOOKS *Books*
☎ 0 2664 8554; 3rd fl, the Emporium, btwn Soi 22 & Soi 24, Th Sukhumvit; 🕙 10.30am-10pm 🚇 Phrom Phong
A smaller version of the Siam Paragon anchor (p84), this Kinokuniya Books branch has a sizable collection of children's books and magazines.

### 📷 L'ARCADIA *Antiques*
☎ 0 2259 9595; 12/2 Soi 23, Th Sukhumvit; 🕙 9am-10pm; 🚇 Asoke
The buyer at L'Arcadia has a sharp eye for collectibles from Burma, Cambodia and Thailand. The extensive range includes Sukhothai cabinets, cute red-lacquer containers, Khmer-style sandstone figures and carved, wooden temple decorations. If you simply can't resist that Burmese lounge chair, the shop can arrange to have it shipped home.

### 📷 NANDAKWANG *Handicrafts*
☎ 0 2258 1962; 108/3 Soi 23, Th Sukhumvit; 🕙 9am-5pm Mon-Sat & 10am-5pm Sun; 🚇 Nana; ♿
A Chiang Mai-based outfit, Nandakwang's products are utterly cute without being cheesy. From woven drinks coasters to embroidered stuffed animals and rugged leather-bottomed satchels, these gifts whisper Thailand without screaming second-rate. There's another branch located on the 4th floor of the Siam Discovery Centre (p88).

L'Arcadia, an antiques wonderland

### 🏠 NICKERMANN'S TAILORS
*Tailor*
☎ 0 2252 9444; basement, Landmark Hotel, 138 Th Sukhumvit; 🕐 10am-9pm; 🚇 Nana; ♿
Corporate ladies rave about Nickermann's tailor-made power suits: pants and jackets that suit curves and busts. Formal ball gowns are another area of expertise.

### 🏠 PHU FA *Handicrafts*
☎ 0 2650 3311; cnr Th Sukhumvit & Soi 7; 🕐 10am-8pm Mon-Fri & 10am-6pm Sat-Sun; 🚇 Nana
Gifts with a cause make that fuzzy feeling fuzzier. This new outlet sells products from HRH Princess Srindhorn's economic development programme for rural villagers. The Thai-made products are mainly kid-friendly: notebooks, change purses and handwoven Karen textiles.

### 🏠 PLAYGROUND!
*Shopping Centre*
☎ 0 2714 7888; www.playgroundstore.co.th; 818 Soi 55, Th Sukhumvit; 🕐 10am-10pm; 🚇 Thong Lor, change to red soi bus
Bangkok's latest trend in concept malls line Thong Lor (Soi 55) as if auditioning for a new boy band. Playground is the street-smart cool one with alt-art books, graffiti displays, vinyl dolls and clothes too hip for professionals.

### 🏠 PROPAGANDA *Décor*

**Emporium, btwn Soi 22 & 24, Th Sukhumvit;** ⏱ **10.30am-9pm;** 🚇 **Phrom Phong**
Housewares and design pieces with an attitude and by local designers can be found at this shop. Also at Siam Discovery Center (p88).

### 🏠 RAJA'S FASHIONS *Tailor*

☎ **0 2253 8379; 1/6 Soi 4, Th Sukhumvit;** ⏱ **10.30am-8pm Mon-Sat;** 🚇 **Nana;** ♿
Raja's thrives on a top-notch reputation for men's tailoring (it seems to have besuited Bangkok's entire US expat population). Just

wait for the final fitting when Raja will tell you, like every one of your predecessors, 'You came in good looking and now you're looking good'. Why change a winning formula?

### 🏠 RASI SAYAM *Handicrafts*

☎ **0 2258 4195; Soi 33, 82 Th Sukhumvit;** ⏱ **9am-5.30pm Mon-Sat;** 🚇 **Asoke**
Once you tire of souvenir kitsch, head straight to Rasi Sayam for tasteful *objets d'art*. Based in a Thai house, it sells delicate woven wall-hangings and intricate baskets, as well as pottery and sandstone statues.

Thai-vegetarian fare that's worth the wait at Atlanta Coffee Shop

# 🍴 EAT

If you chose wisely, you can eat fabulously along this leggy street. A veritable UN of restaurants caters to compatriots and cultured Thais with diplomatic success.

## 🍴 ANA'S GARDEN *Thai* $$
☎ 0 2391 1762; 67 Soi 55, Th Sukhumvit; ⏱ 5am-midnight; 🚈 Thong Lor
A nod to the past, this outdoor garden restaurant is anything but stuffy. The clientele are the swish set of Thong Lor who never start a night without a table full of fiery Thai dishes. Amid the greenery you can pretend that concrete hasn't yet been invented.

## 🍴 ATLANTA COFFEE SHOP *Thai* $
☎ 0 2252 6069; 78 Soi 2, Th Sukhumvit; ⏱ 7am-midnight; 🚈 Ploenchit; 🚻 🚹 V
We could rave until the water buffalo come home. Not only is this the ultimate in impeccably preserved retro coffee shops but it also takes its vegetarian Thai food seriously. Don't miss the stir-fried morning-glory or the breakfasts.

## 🍴 BAANYA *Thai* $$
☎ 0 2251 6439; Soi 7, Th Sukhumvit; ⏱ 11am-11pm; 🚈 Ploenchit; 🚻 🚹
You might lose hope as you walk past the tourist-driven bratwurst-

### STRICTLY VEGETARIAN
It's tough to be truly vegetarian at Thai restaurants. You can ask for 'no meat or seafood' but then your dish arrives with fish sauce. But you won't need to worry at strictly vegetarian places such as Arawy (p60) and Tamarind Café (p133) or Indian restaurants such as Dosa King (p130) and Indian Hut (p103). Don't miss Chinatown during its annual Vegetarian Festival.

and-pasta joints of Sukhumvit's girlie-bar scene but deep inside this *soi* is a genuine Thai restaurant known by a handful of office workers and nosh-explorers. The menu seems straightforward but there are in fact many unique twists, including *lâap kǔaytǐaw* (a spicy meat salad stuffed into rice-flour noodles) and *plaa tub tim* (tilapia).

## 🍴 BED SUPPERCLUB *International* $$$$
☎ 0 2651 3537; 26 Soi 11, Th Sukhuvmit; ⏱ three seatings per evening; 🚈 Nana
When it comes to the much lauded 'fusion' fare, Bangkok is splitting wood not the atom. Thankfully Bed will rescue educated eaters from the mad scientists. Within this sleek and futuristic setting – beds instead of tables and projected art films instead of mood music – the food stands

up to the distractions with a changing menu described as New American with Asian accents. Keep in mind that reservations are essential.

## 🍴 CABBAGES & CONDOMS
*Thai*                                    $$
☎ 0 2229 4611; Soi 12, Th Sukhumvit; 🕙 11am-10pm; 🚇 Asoke; 🚹 🍴 🅥
It isn't the best Thai food in town, but it is the best cause around. Cabbages & Condoms is affiliated with the Population & Community Development Association (PDA), a sex-education/AIDS-prevention organisation credited for Thailand's speedy reaction to the AIDS crisis. In addition to meal names that would make an adolescent chuckle, diners get packaged condoms in lieu of after-dinner mints.

## 🍴 CREPES & CO
*French-Moroccan*              $$$
☎ 0 2653 3990; 18/1 Soi 12, Th Su-khumvit; 🕙 9am- midnight; 🚇 Asoke; 🍴 🅥
Chic without being pretentious, this breezy café is yuppie Bang-kok's favourite brunch date. At Crepes & Co you'll tuck into deli-cate, platter-sized crepes stuffed with such delights as smoky bacon and woodsy mushrooms as well as lots of thick coffee to soothe your Asian exile.

## 🍴 DOSA KING
*Indian-Vegetarian*                $$
☎ 0 2651 1651; 265/1 Soi 19, Th Sukhumvit; 🕙 11am-11pm; 🚇 Asoke; 🍴 🅥
You don't have to get all 'dhal-ed' up to dine on tasty Indian food. (Although a spiffy look would put you in league with the sari-wrapped mothers and clubbing teenagers.) Divine renditions of the Punjabi speciality, *dosa* (a thin, stuffed crepe), adorn the tables like ancient parchment scrolls.

## 🍴 GIUSTO *Italian*            $$$
☎ 0 2258 4321; www.giustobangkok .com; 16 Soi 23, Th Sukhumvit; 🕙 11.30am-2pm & 6pm-10.30pm; 🚇 Asoke; 🚹
Sophisticated simplicity decor-ates the interior and the menu of this contemporary Italian restaurant. The Italian triumvirate of olive oil, lemon and garlic

### BREAKFAST IS SERVED
Thailand's interpretation of Western-style breakfast is sometimes in name only, but the effort is both filling and amusing. Wake up in the past at the retro Atlanta Coffee Shop (p129) and **Federal Hotel coffee shop** (Soi 11, Th Sukhumvit). Or retreat to a Western gourmet microcosm at Kuppa (p132) and Crepes & Co (left).

## WHAT'S YOUR POISON?

The heat might make you gulp down gallons of water during the day, but when it comes to dinnertime toast your meal with spirit. Beer is a tasty complement to Thai food and can cut through the famous chilli sting. Pilsner-style beers are the usual choices: from locally brewed Singha (pronounced 'sing') to imported Heineken. An ingenious but provincial custom is the addition of ice cubes to glasses of beer in order to keep the beverage cool. For the sophisticates, though, wine is the only respectable tableside date, even though it tends to skunk in Bangkok's hellish climate. Wine is best ordered from places that have dedicated cellars and are able to ensure temperature control from port to table.

coaxes freshly grilled fish into an orchestra of flavours, not a mosh pit. The 'name-that-flavour' eater will find contentment without entering a food coma. Come for the set lunch specials (520/590B 2/3 courses).

### 🍴 GREYHOUND CAFE
*International*                    $$$
☎ 0 2664 8663; 2nd fl, Emporium, btwn Soi 22 & Soi 24, Th Sukhumvit; ⏱ 11am-10pm; 🚇 Phrom Phong; ♿ Ⓥ
Don't be fooled by the flimsy fashionista types picking at their pasta and the minimalism *du jour* of the design. The Greyhound Cafe is undoubtedly a very cool place to be seen and the Thai and fusion dishes match the star power. Also at Central Chitlom (p90).

### 🍴 HORNG AHAAN 55
*Thai-Chinese*                     $$
☎ 0 2391 2021; 1087-1091 Th Sukhumvit; ⏱ 6-11pm; 🚇 Thong Lor; ♿ 👶 Ⓥ

The metro magazines will try to steer you to the latest 'white-linen' hotties, but Bangkok's real culinary beefcakes are these naked little store fronts. The décor is almost institutional: besides the essentials there's also a gaudy Chinese shrine and photographs of revered monks. But this leaves more energy and resources for the food, such as saffron-spiked *poo phàt phông ka-rii* (crab curry).

### 🍴 KALPAPRUEK ON FIRST
*Thai-Italian*                     $$
☎ 0 2664 8410; 1st fl, Emporium, Th Sukhumvit; ⏱ 11am-9pm; 🚇 Phrom Phong; ♿
This is the restaurant that many overseas Thais dreamed of having in their cream-and-pasta host countries. All the delicacies of Europe, these exiles must have mused, are missing fish sauce and chillies. These guiding flavours have formed Bangkok's unique interpretation of fusion: spaghetti

with anchovies and chillies and spicy Thai salads with apples. Also on Th Pramuan (p104).

### ⊕ KUPPA International $$$
☎ 0 2663 0495; 39 Soi 16, Th Sukhumvit; ⏱ 10.30am-10.30pm Tue-Sun; 🚇 Asoke; ♿ Ⓥ

Kuppa can pull off all the dishes you thought untranslatable: cream sauces, sophisticated desserts and recognisable cuts of meat. Catch it at weekend brunch when affluent thirty-somethings get delivered in chauffeured BMWs.

### ⊕ NASIR AL-MASRI Egyptian $$
☎ 0 2253 5582; 4/6 Soi 3/1, Th Sukhumvit; ⏱ 7am-4am; 🚇 Nana; ♿ ♨

If there was ever a place to wear your sunglasses at night, Nasir al-Masri is it. With reflective surfaces everywhere, Nasir creates an illusion of oil-money banquets involving artistically arranged sesame-freckled flatbread, creamy hummus and flawlessly fried falafels.

### ⊕ PIZZERIA BELLA NAPOLI Italian $$
☎ 0 2259 0405; 3/3 Soi 31, Th Sukhumvit; ⏱ 6pm-1am Mon-Fri, noon-5pm Sat & Sun; 🚇 Phrom Phong; ♿ ♨ Ⓥ

An eclectic and boisterous crowd gulps down glasses of blood-red wine and gooey, garlicky, wood-

### ONE FOR THE ROAD
After the official closing time, the bleary-headed wander into the night looking for one more bar stool before bed. Stumbling distance from Sukhumvit's club scene is a bar generically called Sukhumvit 11 (we're told just to follow the crowd) and Sin Bar (p134). Off-the-beaten-path is Wong's Place (p117), an old backpacker hang-out. Young Thais prolong the night at open-air restaurants on Soi 4, Th Ratchadaphisek (Mapp140–1, E5).

fired pizzas in this Neapolitan outpost. Prepare to feel horribly jealous when the party next to you orders the prosciutto-bridge pizza.

### ⊕ RUEN-MALLIKA Thai $$$
☎ 0 2663 3211; sub-soi off Soi 22, Th Sukhumvit; ⏱ 11am-11pm; 🚇 Asoke; ♿

Thais have tourists figured out: just convert an old teak house into a restaurant and the crowds will come, regardless of the food. But Ruen-Mallika greatly improves the formula by serving up exquisite dishes, such as spicy *náam phrík* (a thick dipping sauce with vegetables and herbs) and a soulful dish of chicken wrapped in pandanus leaves. Approach Ruen-Mallika by heading along Soi 16, located off Th Ratchadaphisek.

## SOI 38 NIGHT MARKET
*Thai-Chinese* $

Soi 38, Th Sukhumvit; 6pm-3am;
Thong Lor;
What's a night-owl to do when
all the bars close up at 2am?
Never fear, the good old night
market is here. Chow your way to
sobriety with a bowl of *kŭaytĭaw
mŭu daeng* (red pork noodles)
or *kŭaytĭaw lawt* (Chinese-style
spring rolls).

## TAMARIND CAFÉ
*International Vegetarian* $$$

0 2663 7421; 27 Soi 20, Th Sukhumvit;
11am-11pm; Asoke; V
Tamarind Café creates harmoni-
ous unions out of international
ingredients, without ever visiting
the butcher shop. Invite deep-fried
oyster mushrooms escorted by a
sweet Thai dipping sauce to your
table, or pucker up to a fresh fruit
juice. The upstairs terrace is perfect
for a nightcap. Tamarind shares its
space with Gallery F-Stop.

## VIENTIANE KITCHEN
*Northeastern Thai* $$

0 2258 6171; 8 Soi 36, Th Sukhumvit;
11am-midnight; Thong Lor;
Want to catch some local dance
and music but don't want a
canned performance with lousy
food? This open-air barn is alive
with the music of Isan (northeast
Thailand) and such authentic
specialities as *lâap mŭu* (minced
pork salad), *kài yâang* (grilled
marinated chicken) and sticky
rice – all of which can be eaten
with your hands.

# DRINK
## CHEAP CHARLIE'S *Bar*
sub-soi off Soi 11, Th Sukhumvit;
5pm-midnight Mon-Sat;
Nana;
Wild West meets corporate expat
at this wooden beer stall, boasting the cheapest brews on Soi 11.
Bangkok becomes a road-tested

### SHORT-TERM CHAUFFEURS
Strolling Sukhumvit's *soi* that branch off the main avenue can be a real drag. There's no clear footpath, shade or safety from speeding cars. And if you look around, only foreigners and pushcart vendors even try walking these obstacle courses. Thais hop aboard the motorcycle taxis that sit at the mouth of the *soi* just for this purpose. You too can be spared from heat exhaustion by naming your destination or the point within the *soi* – *soot soi* (end of the *soi*), *glaang soi* (middle of the soi) or *bpaak soi* (mouth of the *soi*) – and climbing aboard the back of the bike. These little hops cost 10B; don't bother to ask the price as some drivers will be creative with their answers.

NEIGHBOURHOODS

SUKHUMVIT

## HAIRY SITUATION
Bangkok is all about hair. The socialites wear it long and straight without a hint of frizz. They worship at the various salons owned by Somsak Chulachol, stylists to the stars, including **Salon de Bkk** ( ☎ 0 2664 8880; 1st fl, Emporium, Soi 24, Th Sukhumvit; ☼ 10am-9pm). The hip teens go for that special breed of Asian mullet at **Chic Club** (Map p81, B2; ☎ 0 2658 4147; Soi 5, Siam Square, Th Phra Ram I; ☼ 10am-8pm). For the no-nonsense gals, there's reliable **First Ave Beauty Salon** ( ☎ 0 2252 4780; 4 Soi 1, Th Sukhumvit; ☼ 10am-8pm Fri-Wed), where you get a sensible do and a nice chat.

buddy after you down a few bottles of Singha, sweat through your shirt and argue politics with some know-it-all Euro.

### ▼ KOI *Bar*
☎ 0 2258 1590; 26 Soi 20, Th Sukhumvit; ☼ 8pm-midnight; ◉ Asoke or Phrom Phong
The bar of this trendy sushi restaurant is packed with models posing as if real life were a photo shoot. The convergence of so much eye candy is no accident, Koi lures in card-carrying models with freebies, creating a spectacle in its own right.

### ▼ SIN BAR *Bar*
☎ 0 9501 6735; 18 Soi 4/Nana, Th Sukhumvit; ☼ 9pm-till late; ◉ Nana
Technically an 'entertainment' complex, Sin Bar is Nana's alter ego: three floors divided into a pool hall, dance club and rooftop bar all noticeably lacking in the *soi*'s namesake industry, prostitutes. Reliably sneaking past the

curfew restrictions, the rooftop bar is the after-party scene for clubbers and night owls not hunting for 'hello handsums'.

## ★ PLAY
As a play date for the non-Nana tourist, Sukhumvit is known for its DJ clubs and day spas.

### ▣ BAAN THAI WELLNESS RETREAT *Spa*
☎ 0 2258 5403; thebaanthai.com; 7 Soi 32, Th Sukhumvit; à la carte from 1500B, lodging-spa packages from US$770; ☼ 10am-6pm; ◉ Thong Lor; ♿
This former mansion has reinvented itself as a spa retreat, where rest and relaxation are encased in one scenic package. Accommodation is in handsomely decorated traditional teak houses, while spa treatments include a personal consultation for determining your Ayurvedic body type. A large range of facilities including beauty salon, meditation pavilion and gym.

See and be seen at popular Q Bar (p136)

## ⭐ BED SUPPERCLUB
*Dance Club*

☎ 0 2651 3537; www.bedsupperclub
.com; 26 Soi 11, Th Sukhumvit; ⏰ 8pm-
1am; 🚇 Nana

All white but not virginal, Bed
Supperclub compliments its
fine-dining side with a separate
club devoted to resident and international DJs. Famous spinners
and hot theme nights keep Bed
on clubbers' checklists.

## ⭐ BUATHIP THAI MASSAGE
*Massage*

☎ 0 2251 2627; 4/1-2 Soi 5, Th Sukhumvit; ⏰ 10am-midnight; 🚇 Nana; ♿
Buathip has long been known for
its blind masseuses, who will give

you a strong and intuitive treatment. It's a low-key place favoured
by Thai regulars and expats.

## ⭐ DVN SPA & WELLBEING
CENTER *Spa*

☎ 0 2261 4818; www.dvn-wellbeing
.com; 8 Soi 35, Th Sukhumvit; day
packages from 1600B, 100min; ⏰ 10am-
10pm; 🚇 Phrom Phong

Travel globally, spa locally. DVN
emphasises Thai massage and
body scrubs as well as exotic
beauty treatments. The menu
might look familiar but the setting
is touchingly Thai: an atmospheric
wooden house and lush garden so
typical of the Sukhumvit estates.
Its sister property is Divana Spa

## A DATE WITH A DOCTOR

Most holidays hope not to end up in the hospital, but these days Thailand has become a destination for medical treatments, from hip replacements to nips and tucks. It's cheaper, offers better service and often more sophisticated technology. Here are a few of the hospitals that cater to Western tourists.

**Bumrungrad Hospital** (Map p122-3, A1; ☎ 0 2667 1000; www.bumrungrad.com; 33 Soi 3, Th Sukhumvit; ℝ Nana) blends five-star service and hotel-style accommodation with US-managed and -accredited medical facilities.

**BNH** (Map p113, A4; ☎ 0 2632 0550; www.bnhhospital.com; Th Convent; ℝ Sala Daeng, ☺ Silom) is well-regarded for general medicine and dental procedures.

**Dental Hospital** (Map p122-3, F3; ☎ 0 2260 5000; www.dentalhospitalbangkok.com; 88/88 Soi 49, Th Sukhumvit; ℀ 9am-8pm Mon-Sat, 9am-4pm Sun ℝ Phrom Phong) is a private dental clinic that covers regular check-ups, filings and root canals.

**St Carlos Medical Spa** ( ☎ 0 2975 6700; www.stcarlos.com; 5/84 Moo 2, Th Tiwanon, Banklang, Pathum Thani) is for the non-celebrity hooked on celebrity treatments, such as detoxifying and fasting programmes using traditional Thai medicines and massage.

**Yanhee Hospital** (Map pp140-1, A2; ☎ 0 2879 0300, ext 1047; www.yanhee.net; Th Charoen Sanit Wong, near Phra Ram VII bridge) is a blessing for every Tom, Dick and Harry who'd rather be Jane. The hospital specialises in sex reassignment and chondroplasty (shaving of the Adam's apple) without the long waiting lists that accompany such procedures overseas.

( ☎ 0 2661 6784; 7 Soi 25, Th Sukhumvit).

### 🌟 LIVING ROOM Live Music
☎ 0 264 9888; Sheraton Grande Sukhumvit, 250 Th Sukhumvit, btwn Soi 12 & Soi 14; ℀ 9pm-midnight; ℝ Asoke; ℅

We'll come clean – the Living Room is a hotel buffet restaurant. But where most of its ilk are sedated by corny covers bands, this cosy upmarket place is alive with the grooves of some of the top jazz acts around. The mellow Sunday brunch starts at around 11am.

### 🌟 Q BAR Dance Club
☎ 0 2252 3274; www.qbarbangkok .com; 34 Soi 11, Th Sukhumvit; ℀ 8pm-2am; ℝ Nana; ℅ fair

The club that introduced Bangkok to the lounge scene in 1999 is still alive and writhing. This darkened industrial space sees a revolving cast of somebodies, nobodies and working girls. Various theme nights fill the weekly calendar.

### 🌟 RASAYANA RETREAT Spa
☎ 0 2662 4803; www.rasayanaretreat .com; 57 Soi Prommit off Soi 39, Th Sukhumvit; à la carte from 1500B; ℀ 10am-7pm; ℝ Phrom Phong

The latest generation of spa facilities, Rasayana combines basic beauty and massage treatments with holistic healing techniques, such as detoxification, colonic irrigation and hypnotherapy.

⭐ **SFX CINEMA** *Cinema*
☎ 0 2260 9333; Emporium, 6th fl, Th Sukhumvit, btwn Soi 22 & Soi 24; 🚇 Phrom Phong; ♿ ⚥
On the top floor of the Emporium shopping centre, this cinema serves up the usual Hollywood shoot-and-snog standards. But

this cinema stands out because of its fab sound and projection quality.

⭐ **WORLD FELLOWSHIP OF BUDDHISTS** *Meditation*
☎ 0 2661 1284; www.wfb-hq.org; Benjasiri Park, Soi 24, Th Sukhumvit; free admission; 🚇 Phrom Phong; ♿
On the first Sunday of the month, this centre of Theravada Buddhism hosts meditation classes in English from 2pm to 5.30pm. The fellowship also holds interesting forums on Buddhist issues.

# >GREATER BANGKOK

Outside central Bangkok, the neighbourhoods become more Thai and more suburban, meaning that fewer commercial signs are in roman script and the roads become highways and flyovers. One concentration of community can be found near Victory Monument, a large traffic circle pinned by a memorial to an obscure Siamese victory over the French. In the shadow of the Victory Monument Skytrain station is a night market that feeds and clothes many Thai students who live nearby. The elevated walkway that nearly circumnavigates the intersection is treated like a university quad for catwalking youth fashions.

The last stop on the northern extension of the Skytrain line is the mother of all markets: Chatuchak Weekend Market, the sole reason most tourists venture beyond the city centre. Across the street you'll find fruit and veg galore at Aw Taw Kaw Market. Another suburban draw is RCA (Royal City Avenue), a strip mall of nightclubs currently dominating the city's social calendar.

## GREATER BANGKOK

### 👁 SEE
| | | |
|---|---|---|
| Baiyoke Sky Tower | 1 | C5 |
| Bangkok Doll Factory & Museum | 2 | D5 |
| Children's Discovery Museum | 3 | D2 |
| Lettuce Farm Palace | 4 | C5 |
| Tadu Contemporary Art | 5 | F4 |
| Victory Monument | 6 | C5 |

### 🏠 SHOP
| | | |
|---|---|---|
| Chatuchak Weekend Market | 7 | D2 |
| Ratchada Market | 8 | E2 |

### 🍴 EAT
| | | |
|---|---|---|
| Aw Taw Kaw Market | 9 | D2 |
| Pickle Factory | 10 | D5 |
| Reflections Bar & Restaurant | 11 | D4 |
| Spring | 12 | E6 |

### 🍸 DRINK
| | | |
|---|---|---|
| ICY | 13 | D3 |
| Tawandaeng | 14 | D8 |

### ⭐ PLAY
| | | |
|---|---|---|
| Club Astra | 15 | F5 |
| House of Dhamma | 16 | E2 |
| Raintree Pub | 17 | C5 |
| Santika | 18 | F7 |
| Saxophone Pub & Restaurant | 19 | C5 |
| Thailand Cultural Centre | 20 | E4 |
| Zeta | (see 15) | |

Please see over for map

# ⊙ SEE

## ⊙ BAIYOKE SKY TOWER

☎ 0 2656 3000; 222 Baiyoke Hotel, Th Ratchaprarop; admission incl access to 77th, 83rd & 84th fl 200B; ☀ 10.30am-10pm; 🚇 Phayathai, 🚌 504, 513; ♿
It's a bird; it's a crane; no, it's the Baiyoke Sky Hotel, the nation's tallest scraper, measuring a gangly 88 storeys (309m tall). On the 84th floor is a revolving observation deck, something akin to a geriatric carnival ride. This is the only sky-high perch in Bangkok geared towards families.

## ⊙ BANGKOK DOLL FACTORY & MUSEUM

☎ 0 2245 3008; www.bangkokdolls .com; 85 Soi Ratchataphan, Th Ratchaprarop; admission free; ☀ 8am-5pm Mon-Sat; 🚌 taxi; ♿
New and antique dolls dressed in national costumes are displayed for appreciation, while the gift shop sells onsite factory-made dolls, a unique industry that helped preserve Thai traditional costumes in miniature. The museum is difficult to find; the best approach is from Th Sri Ayuthaya heading east.

## ⊙ CHILDREN'S DISCOVERY MUSEUM

☎ 0 2615 7333; Queen Sirikit Park, Th Kamphaeng Phet 4; ☀ 9am-5pm Tue-

### WORTH THE TRIP
You'll need to plan ahead and, gasp, leave the comfort of central Bangkok to reach the **Prasart Museum** (☎ 0 2379 3601; 9 Soi Krungthepkretha 4a, Th Krung Thepkretha, Bang Kapi; admission 500B; ☀ 10.30am-3pm Tue-Sun by appointment; 🚌 92). Prasart Vongsakul's collection of traditional buildings and antiques is a must for any die-hard art and architecture fan. It's tricky to get to so call ahead for directions and let them know you're coming. The trip will take about an hour.

Fri, 10am-6pm Sat & Sun; 100/50B; 🚇 Mo Chit, ⊙ Chatuchak Park; ♿
Through hands-on activities, learning is well disguised as fun. Kids can stand inside a bubble or see how an engine works. Most activities are geared to children aged five to 10. There is also a toddler-suitable playground at the back of the main building. You'll find the Children's Discovery Museum opposite Chatuchak Weekend Market.

## ⊙ LETTUCE FARM PALACE

☎ 0 2245 4934; Th Si Ayuthaya, near Th Ratchaprarop; 100B; ☀ 9am-4pm; 🚇 Phayathai, 🚌 513, 63, 72
Of Bangkok's traditional house museums, Lettuce Farm Palace is a nice counterpoint to Jim Thompson's house. The displays are less

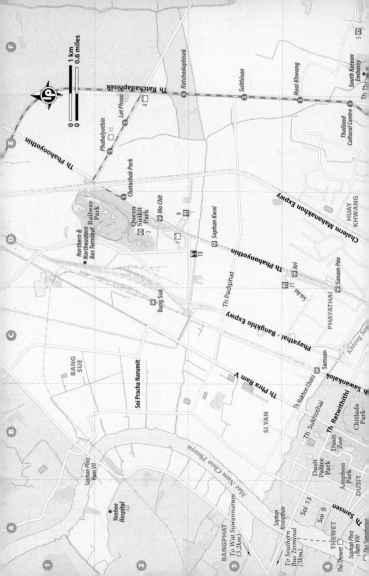

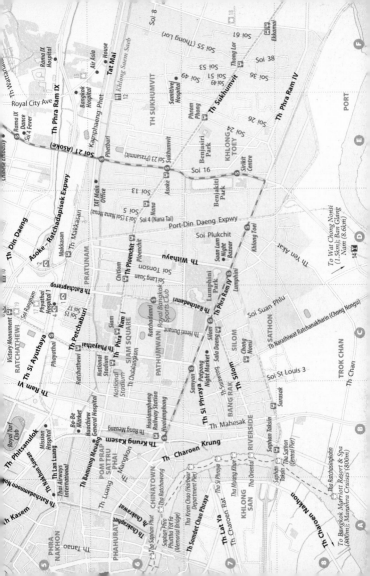

formal, allowing enough room to wander and wonder. There are six traditional wooden houses filled with Thai art and knick-knacks, including pottery from Bronze-Age Ban Chiang, masks from the *khon* dance-drama and traditional musical instruments. The most famous exhibit is the Lacquer Pavilion, which was moved here from a monastery near Ayuthaya and is decorated with intricate gold-leaf and black-lacquer *Jataka* (stories of the Buddha) and *Ramakian* murals. The palace grounds were once a farm and, later, the home of Princess Chumbon of Nakhon Sawan.

### ◎ TADU CONTEMPORARY ART

☎ 0 2645 2473; www.tadu.net; Barcelona Motors Bldg, 7th fl, 99/2 Th Thiam Ruammit; 🕙 10am-6pm Mon-Sat; 🚕 taxi; ♿

One of the major nexus of art, culture and conversation, Tadu focuses on contemporary exhibits, theatre, dance and avant-garde performances. It also collaborates with various film organisations promoting Thai cinema.

### ◎ VICTORY MONUMENT

**Th Ratchawithi & Phayathai; 🚇 Victory Monument**
A busy traffic circle revolves around this obelisk that commemorates a 1939 Thai victory against the French in Laos. An elevated walkway circumnavigates the roundabout, funnelling the pedestrian traffic in and out of the Skytrain station as well as providing a gathering spot for breakdancers, flirting gangs of guys and gals, and lots of fashion experiments. Because Victory

Going 'round in circles – Skytrain, pedestrians and road traffic converge at Victory Monument

Upmarket bag ladies, Chatuchak Weekend Market

Monument is outside the core of Bangkok, the neighbourhood is less cosmopolitan and more reminiscent of provincial towns elsewhere in the country.

# SHOP
## CHATUCHAK WEEKEND MARKET *Market*
☎ 0 2272 4440; bounded by Th Kamphaeng Phet, Chatuchak Park & Th Phahonyothin; ⏰ 8am-6pm Sat & Sun; 🚇 Mo Chit, 🚉 Chatuchak Park
You've got to see it to believe it: this weekend market is a veritable village of vendor stalls selling clothes, décor, junk and collectibles. It is the number one shopping destination in the city despite the heat and crowds. For more information, see p17.

## RATCHADA MARKET
*Market*
intersection of Th Ratchada & Th Lad Phrao; ⏰ 6pm-midnight Sat; 🚇 Lad Phrao or Ratchadaphisek
Most night markets are dominated by knock-off Louis Vuitton but this one fancies vintage and Vespas instead. In Thailand, Vespas were once only workhorses used to deliver bolts of linoleum, but a boho crew of Thais have joined the global trend of outfitting these

retro scooters as portable fashion accessories and this weekly flea market is both their supply house and showroom.

#  EAT

## AW TAW KAW MARKET
*Thai-Chinese* $

**Th Kampangphet;** ☼ **10am-5pm;** ⊗ **Chatuchak Park;** ♿

Across the street from Chatuchak Market, Aw Taw Kaw is one of Bangkok's biggest fruit and agricultural markets, selling what many swear are the tastiest pomelos around. Next to the produce vendors are food stalls that earn equal veneration for duck curries and other street treats.

## BAN GLANG NAM
*Thai-Chinese* $$$

☎ **0 2292 0175; 288 Soi 14, Th Phra Ram III;** ☼ **11am-10.30pm;** 🚕 **taxi;** ♿

There are tons of riverside restaurants but none have the old-fashioned charm of rickety Ban Glang Nam. With views of riverside industry instead of manicured temples, Ban Glang Nam feels many nautical knots away from the tourist machine. Foreigners are usually brought here by Thai friends who fill the table with dishes of whole grilled fish, *tôm yam kûng* (spicy soup with shrimp) and other seafood dishes.

## PICKLE FACTORY
*International* $$

☎ **0 2246 3036 55; Soi 2, Th Ratchawithi, Victory Monument;** ☼ **5.30-11.30pm;** 🚇 **Victory Monument;** ♿ 🚶 Ⓥ

This converted modern house rolls out homemade pizzas to a practised crowd of layabouts. East-meets-West pizzas defy conventional wisdom with combos such as *khîi mao* (wing beans and holy basil) and pizza vodka (yup, those are peas). Take a taxi from the station to avoid a long, lonely walk.

## REFLECTIONS BAR & RESTAURANT *Pan Asian* $$

☎ **0 2270 3340; 81 Soi Ari, Th Phahonyothin;** ☼ **11am-11pm;** 🚇 **Ari**

Kitted out in candy colours, this darling of Soi Ari wowed Thai menu-crawlers several years ago and still maintains their attention. The options ramble from Chinese seafood to Thai standards and this place is a welcome touch of style for hole-in-the-wall fans. The attached hotel lobby-bar is a favourite with indie creatives.

## SPRING
*Thai-international* $$$

☎ **0 2392 2747; 199 Soi 2/Soi Promsri, Th Sukhumvit;** ☼ **11am-2.30pm & 5.30-11pm;** 🚕 **taxi**

In the dry season, this fashionable restaurant spreads its guests out on the lawn for alfresco wining and dining. To soak up a garden ambience in urban Bangkok is as luxurious as the chocolate desserts.

#  DRINK

## ▼ ICY *Bar*
☎ 0 2272 4775; Th Kamphaengphet; ☽ 6pm-1am; 🚕 taxi

For a little something different, intrepid gays haul themselves out to the mainly Thai scene near Chatuchak. Young college students, swilling cheap beers and whiskey, mingle to the beat of Thai pop.

## ▼ TAWANDAENG *Bar*
☎ 0 2678 1114; 462/61 Th Phra Ram III, cnr Th Narathiwat Ratchanakharin; ☽ 6pm-1am; 🚕 taxi; ♿

Seeking a more local feel than your average expat bar? You asked for it – Tawandaeng is a massive beer hall and German-style microbrewery *(rong beer)*. Between sets of sing-along pop tunes, choruses of 'Happy Birthday' erupt from the overcrowded tables.

# ★ PLAY

## ☆ CLUB ASTRA *Dance Club*
☎ 0 2622 2572; www.club-astra.com; Block C, Royal City Ave, Th Phra Ram IX; ☽ 10pm-2am; 🚕 taxi

Credited for diversifying teen-scream RCA, Club Astra pulls in the Thai indie crowd, backpackers and expats for international DJs sans gimmicks. If the joint isn't jumping then check out the surrounding RCA clubs blasting radio rap and commercial pop.

## ☆ HOUSE OF DHAMMA *Meditation*
☎ 0 2511 0439; www.houseofdhamma.com; 26/9 Soi 15, Th Lat Phrao; suggested donation 300B; ☽ regular sessions 10.30am every 2nd & 3rd Sun; 🚇 Lat Phrao

This meditation centre north of central Bangkok offers meditation retreats and classes in *vipassana* (insight meditation). A two-day introduction course is geared towards beginners and held four times a year. Sessions are in English.

---

## FLYING SOLO
If you've ascended to the City of Angels without a companion, then make two distinct lines. Men over here in line A; women, line B.

Line A: Welcome to paradise, where beautiful women will throw themselves at you, all for a modest sum (either monetary or status). Line B: For better or worse, you will be virtually invisible except at a few neighbourhood spots: Ad Here the 13th (p64), Café Trio (p91) and Cheap Charlie's (p133).

## ⭐ MANOHRA CRUISES COOKING COURSES
*Cooking School*

☎ 0 2476 0022 Bangkok Marriott Resort & Spa, Th Charoen Nakhorn, Thonburi; minimum four people 2000B; 🕑 9am-noon; 🚢 free shuttle boat from Tha Sathon

Here's a novel idea, whip up a curry while cruising the river at the same time. Classes arranged through Manohra Cruises include a market tour and a cooking lesson aboard a restored rice barge boat. Now that's a mouthful.

## ⭐ RAINTREE PUB
*Bar & Live Music*

☎ 0 2245 7230; 116/63-64 Soi Rangnam, Th Phahonyothin; 🕑 6pm-1am; 🚇 Victory Monument

Decorated like a country-and-western bar with driftwood and buffalo horns, Raintree is a relic in Bangkok's music scene. The nightly bands carry on the 'songs for life' tradition, one of Thailand's most unique adaptations of rock music, that has now passed from current to classic.

## ⭐ SANTIKA
*Dance Club*

☎ 0 2711 5886; 235/11 Soi 63/Ekkamai, Th Sukhumvit; 🕑 9pm-1am

That weekend traffic jam on Ekkamai is feeding into super-sized Santika, a hi-so Thai favourite. Shove yourself into the main dance hall for live bands, or squirm into the hip-hop room. If all else fails, grab an outdoor table with the grown-ups.

## ⭐ SAXOPHONE PUB & RESTAURANT
*Live Music*

☎ 0 2246 5472; www.saxophonepub .com; 3/8 Th Phayathai, Victory Monument; 🕑 6pm-1am; 🚇 Victory Monument; ♿

Saxophone is still Bangkok's premier live music venue, a dark, intimate space where you can pull up a chair just a few metres away from the band and see their every bead of sweat. If you like some mystique in your musicians, watch the blues, jazz, reggae or rock from the balcony.

### WORTH THE TRIP

Granted it is sort of cheating to get culture bundled up at a theme village, but if time and patience is brief, then **Rose Garden Country Resort & Hotel** ( ☎ 0 3432 2544 www.rose-garden.com; KM 32 Th Phetkasem, Nakhon Pathom; accommodation from US$100; 🚗 private car or tour; ♿ ) can introduce the family to many traditional, if staged, aspects of Thai culture (morning religious rituals, rice harvesting, dance and music). There are also elephant rides, botanical gardens and even a golf course.

### Grit "Num" Thammachotika
*DJ, percussionist in Thai reggae band T-Bone*

**Thai or foreign music?** Foreign music, because I learn a lot from listening to it. **Favourite place to buy CDs?** Siam Square (p83). The staff at some of the stores there really know music and can recommend new bands. **Favourite local band?** Teddy Ska, a band that plays ska covers down on Khao San Rd, is really fun. **Favourite place for live music?** Saxophone (opposite) is good for jazz, blues and a change of scene; T-Bone plays there every Friday. **Best club in town?** Tapas (p108). I've DJed there a long time and feel like I know everybody. Bed Supperclub (p135) is also fun; lots of foreigners, and I meet a lot of new people there.

*By Austin Bush*

NEIGHBOURHOODS

GREATER BANGKOK

Hot pink is the new yellow

### ☆ THAILAND CULTURAL CENTRE *Theatre*
☎ 0 2247 0028; Th Ratchadaphisek;
Ⓜ Thailand Cultural Centre; ♿
This top-class, multipurpose arts venue hosts the annual International Festival of Dance & Music in June and other music and drama shows throughout the year. Call for the schedule; their website is out of date and in Thai only. Between Soi Tiam Ruammit & Th Din Daeng.

### ☆ ZETA
*Gay & Lesbian*
☎ 0 2203 0994; 29/67 Block S, Royal City Avenue, Th Phra Ram IX; ⏱ 6pm-1am;
🚕 taxi
All of Bangkok's *tom-dees* (lesbians) complain that there is no dedicated space for girls who love girls. But Zeta has come to the rescue offering an upscale RCA club dedicated to the ladies, including an all-female staff.

Potter from the Mon village of Kwan-A-Man on Ko Kret

# AYUTHAYA

Designated a Unesco World Heritage Site, the temple ruins of Ayuthaya are all that remain of the former capital's illustrious heyday. Before Bangkok rose up from the river basin to become the behemoth city it is today, the Siamese capital sat 85km north of the modern one along the mighty Mae Nam Chao Phraya and enjoyed patronage from the roving sea merchants of the Asian trade route.

The Siamese royal capital flourished from 1350 to 1767 and was named after Ayodhya, the Sanskrit word for 'unassailable' or 'undefeatable', as well as the home of Rama in the Indian epic *Ramayana*. An auspicious name that didn't prevail against the eventual Burmese sacking in 1767 that ended the island city's reign. The invading army looted the city's golden treasures and carted off the royal family as prisoners. The nervous system of the emerging Thai nation fractured into competing factions until General Taksin united the territories and established a new capital near Bangkok a mere three years later. The Burmese eventually abandoned their Thai conquest.

Ayuthaya then developed into a provincial trading town while its once magnificent monuments succumbed to gravity and looters. Over 400 temples were built in the ancient city, now the centre of the modern town. Some of the surviving temples have been restored but very few Buddha images remain intact – due to inoperable war wounds. Today cultural tourists scoot about on bicycles or motorcycles photographing the historical survivors.

Nature sculpted the most famous attraction at **Wat Phra Mahathat** – a sandstone Buddha head embedded in twisted tree roots. The sacred image is doubly auspicious because of the tree's embrace, a physical combination of formal Buddhism and folk animism.

**Wat Ratburana** retains one of the best preserved Khmer-style *prang* (tower) in old Ayuthaya. It was built in the 15th century by King Borom Rachathirat II in honour of his two brothers who died battling each other for the throne.

**Wat Phra Si Sanphet**, the biggest temple of its time, has three surviving stupas in the classic bell-shaped, Ayuthaya style. Built in the late 14th century, the compound was used for important royal ceremonies and once contained a 16m-high standing Buddha (Phra Si Sanphet) covered with 250kg of gold.

In the evenings, many ruin-hoppers take a semicircle **boat ride** (arranged at local guesthouses) around the island with stops at **Wat Phanan Choeng**, a popular pilgrimage destination for Thai-Chinese who come to honour the Chinese explorer Sam Po Kong (Zheng He) who visited the capital in 1407.

Shutterbugs will want to visit **Wat Chai Wattanaram** in time for sunset to catch the silhouette of the Khmer-style *prang* alongside the river. Extensively restored, the temple was built in the 17th century by King Prasat Thong in honour of his mother.

The remainder of the boat ride winds through the riverside communities where meals are cooked, dishes are washed, and TV commercials echo from the banks. The trip ends at the night market, a fixture in the lives of a typical Thai town, despite its ancient pedigree.

## JUST THE FACTS
> Information: **Ayuthaya Tourist Office** ( ☎ 0 3524 6076-7; 108/22 Th Si Sanphet; ☼ 9am-5pm).
> Transport: train from Bangkok's Hualamphong Station (3rd class ticket 20B, 1½ hours, every 30 minutes between 6.20am to 9.30am and 6pm to 10pm); bus from Bangkok's Northern & Northeastern Terminal (45B, 1½ hours, frequent).
> Getting Around: guesthouses on Soi 1, Th Naresuan, rent bicycles and motorbikes. Informal boat tours (from 200B per hour) can be arranged at river piers.

# KO SAMET

Bangkok's beachside playground is a T-bone shaped island of squeaky blonde beaches, glassy water and not a single high-rise – surprisingly rustic considering its proximity to the capital. That doesn't mean this is castaway paradise though; Ko Samet sits solidly on the beaten track with weekend crowds, jet skis, discos, sarong-sellers and beach masseuses. But footpaths skirting the rocky exterior provide mental, if not physical, seclusion.

Before being designated a national park in 1981, Ko Samet claimed literary distinction thanks to Thai poet Sunthorn Phu's epic *Phra Aphaimani*. In this classical poem, a prince was exiled to an undersea kingdom from which a mermaid helped him escape to Ko Samet. This scene is memorialised on the island with a weatherworn statue of the two built on a rocky point separating the sights of Ao Hin Khok and Hat Sai Kaew.

Most boats from the mainland arrive at Na Dan pier, Samet's 'commercial' area filled with a short block of shophouses and rutted roads. A short walk west leads you to **Hat Sai Kaew** (Diamond Beach), the longest and most populous of Ko Samet's beaches. Tucked behind the treeline are moderately priced and average beachside guesthouses. Around the next headland are scruffy **Ao Hin Khok** and **Ao Phai**, two small bays fittingly claimed by backpackers and bars. Ao Phai is beginning a steady image upgrade with some of the older guesthouses transforming into more stylish models. Next in line is **Ao Phutsa**, a nice little curve of sand before a lengthy run of rocky headlands leading to **Ao Wong Deuan**, a beach that resembles the girlie-bar scene of Pattaya, and **Ao Thian** (Candlelight Beach), claimed by Thai college kids and all-night guitar jams. The southern bays of **Ao Wai** and **Ao Kiu Na Nok** are deliciously secluded. Armed with enough water and sunscreen you can follow the oceanfront footpaths as far south as your feet and your stomach will take you.

On the northeastern shores is **Ao Phrao**, dubbed Paradise Beach in English and claimed by two top-end beach resorts and surrounding sea breezes. The resorts waterfront bars are a popular pilgrimage for sunset-watchers and the affiliated spa offers all of the mainland relaxation treatments.

And what should you do amid these jewel-toned waters? Be warned that a beach blanket and book is an invitation for the itinerant merchants to approach multiple times selling massages, sarongs and henna tattoos. A simple 'no thank you' minus a smile is culturally polite and doesn't invite badgering. Beyond sunning and splashing, boat tours head out to coral-filled snorkelling spots, secluded islands and the Turtle Conservation Centre on nearby Ko Man Nai. Dive operators shuttle out to the underwater rock formations of Hin Pholeung, a bit of a trek from Samet.

When your workout is done, you can nibble at freshly caught fish at one of the many beachside barbecues. Then meet and swill with other visitors at the open-air bars that specialise in Red Bull and vodka buckets, a Thai beach concoction.

On weekends and holidays, almost all of Bangkok flocks to Samet's shores, making it difficult to find accommodation upon arrival. More and more Samet is copying the big city convention of using and honouring reservations, a necessity to peak periods.

## JUST THE FACTS

> Information: Ko Samet is 200km southeast of Bangkok and accessible by public bus to the port town of Ban Phe, where boats depart for the island. There is a 400B national park entrance fee.
> Transport: bus from Bangkok's Ekkamai station to Rayong (140B, 2½ hours, every 30 minutes), then sǎwngthǎew (20B, 30 minutes; frequent departures) to Ban Phe, then ferry to Ko Samet (50B, 45 minutes, hourly).
> Accommodation: **Samed Villa** ( ☎ 0 3864 4094; www.samedvilla.com; Ao Phai; bungalows 600-1800B) and **Sametville Resort** ( ☎ 0 3865 1681-82; www .sametvilleresort.com; Ao Wai; bungalows 700-2600B).

# FLOATING MARKETS

In olden times, Central Thai farmers would deliver their goods to market aboard the only transport they owned: the family boat. This old tradition has been widely photographed – slim dugout canoes loaded with brightly coloured fruits and vegetables sidle up to a riverbank dock – but this iconic image is more historical than current. The floating markets that once dotted the canals have been replaced with terrestrial markets and the boats with motorcycles thanks to the advancement of asphalt and cars.

The most famous survivor is **Damnoen Saduak**, which appears on every package tour itinerary. Once one of the largest floating markets in the area, attracting vendors from near and far, today Damnoen Saduak sells more trinkets than bananas. Many tourists are disappointed not to find the old ways in action, but there are some redeeming qualities should you be committed to a visit. Slender longtail boats are the mode of exploration with a requisite stop for a bowl of 'boat noodles', prepared by a canoe cook. Then the real souvenir blitz begins – if you haven't already loaded up on wooden knick-knacks, you're in luck. Beyond the market stalls is further evidence of the riverside life of Central Thais: houses built on stilts along the water's edge and small floating gas stations filling-up thirsty longtail boats.

Across the river from Bangkok in Thonburi is the floating food market of **Taling Chan**. Several docks on Khlong Bangkok Yai carry on the old tradition of floating meals. On either side of the docks are longtail boats outfitted with portable kitchens: charcoal grills for toasting gulf shrimp or whole fish, while other boats balance steaming pots of soup. Diners kick off their shoes and shimmy up to the low tables for a complicated family meal or a quick nibble before picking up fruits and sundries from the roadside vendors.

When Thais feel like reliving the days of yore, they go to **Talat Ban Mai**, an atmospheric riverside market that originated 100 years ago. Today the old-fashioned wooden shophouses teetering on the riverbank are mainly a weekend attraction for local Thais prowling for good eats. Many businesses are owned by the second and third generation of ethnic Teochew Chinese who migrated to Thailand's central plains in search of work. The story of these immigrants is a classic success tale, many arrived with only a suitcase and a few coins in their pocket, labouring on farms and in factories with enough diligence to secure a merchant future for their children and a university education for their grandchildren. The market's Chinese heritage continues with the foods on offer – *kǔay chai* (dumplings stuffed with green veg) and *galorchi* (sweet, deep-fried tapioca patties). A visit here contains all the components for a true Thai outing – food, trinkets, a temple visit, more food. You can combine a trip to the market with a boat tour ( ☎ 0 3851 4333; adult 100B; ☖ hourly 9am-3pm Sat & Sun) along Mae Nam Bang Pakong, beginning at Wat Sothon Wararam Worawihan in Chachoengsao town. From November to February, this brackish river is full of striped catfish that entice hungry dolphins in from the Gulf of Thailand.

## JUST THE FACTS

Damnoen Saduak
> Information: Damnoen Saduak is 70km southwest of Bangkok and is open from 6am to noon, Saturday and Sunday.
> Transport: bus from Thonburi's Southern Bus Terminal (72B, 1½ hours; every 20 minutes from 6.30am); 500-700B for longtail-boat hire at Damnoen Saduak.

Taling Chan:
> Information: Taling Chan is 15km west of Bangkok in Thonburi and is open from 9am to 3pm, Saturday and Sunday.
> Transport: city bus 79 from Th Ratchadamnoen Klang or Ratchaprasong (16B, 45 minutes, frequent).

Talat Ban Mai:
> Information: Talat Ban Mai is in Chachoengsao, 80km east of Bangkok, and is open from 7am to 7pm, Saturday and Sunday.
> Transport: bus from Bangkok's Ekkamai bus station (90B, 1½ hours, frequent departures,) or train from Hualamphong station (15B to 40B, 2 hours, roughly hourly departures) to Chachoengsao (80km east of Bangkok).

# KO KRET

Are your nerves shot from dodging túk-túk and withstanding ear-splitting traffic? As soothing as a trip to a day spa, this island right in the middle of Mae Nam Chao Phraya, is a crafty little getaway in every sense. Ko Kret is known for its distinctive earthen pottery and is home to one of Thailand's oldest settlements of Mon people, who were the dominant ethnic group in central Thailand between the 6th and 10th centuries AD. Today the Mon have all but integrated into Thai society but are still a distinct ethnic group in Burma. Little of the cultural distinction remains here as well, but Ko Kret still retains its ancestral art form on a small scale with local potters using locally dug clay and working in open-air studios sprinkled across the island. Seeing the pieces being crafted – all by hand – promotes what might otherwise seem like a mass-produced souvenir into the more distinguished class of handicraft.

During the week, the car-less island receives relatively few visitors and a leisurely stroll around the Ko Kret's narrow footpaths provides a fascinating contrast to the Big Mango's streetlife. Ko Kret's rush hour may consist of two motorcycles, and the counterparts to Bangkok's fierce *soi* (lane) dogs are now lazy creatures too content to scratch themselves. You'll even spot a water buffalo grazing leisurely under a shade tree.

But on weekends the whole island does a quick change into a serious commercial enterprise when Thais from Bangkok hop across the river for a day's outing of shopping and eating. Souvenir stores dust off their merchandise of Thai-oriented knick-knacks and vendors roll out their carts to serve drinks in portable earthenware jugs or prepare deep-fried flowers, a dish claiming Mon heritage. There are also occasional traditional dance performances on view and family fun.

No outing is complete in Thailand without a temple visit and Ko Kret does not disappoint. Beside the longtail boat pier, a Mon Buddhist temple called Wat Paramai Yikawat, also known simply as 'Wat Mon', contains a Mon-style marble Buddha. Dessert makers and sweet shops also appeal to the visiting appetites and are accessible via the longtail tours that leave Tha Nonthaburi on weekends.

## JUST THE FACTS

> Information: Ko Kret is 17km north of Bangkok.
> Transport: Chao Phraya River Express boat to Tha Nonthaburi, then hire a longtail boat (500B for 2 hours) to Ko Kret, or join a longtail tour (100B per person; 3 hours; weekends only).

# MUANG BORAN & ERAWAN MUSEUM

In the wrong hands, Muang Boran (Ancient City) could have been the Eurodisney of Thailand. But fortunately this enormous open-air museum was shaped by a philanthropist passionate about conserving Thailand's architectural traditions. It's such a genuinely wholesome place – all trimmed gardens, picnicking families and gushing streams – that it will erase any scars suffered in amoral Bangkok.

More than 100 mini-replicas of Thailand's important buildings, including famous temples, traditional houses and monuments, are spread over the 128-hectare site designed in the shape of Thailand, with the attractions occupying the corresponding geographic area of their real-life components. Some all-star features include a recreation of the Grand Palace of Ayuthaya, which was destroyed by the Burmese invasion; Prasat Phimai in Nakhon Ratchasima province; and a handicrafts village.

The intention of the museum isn't to be a shortcut for sightseers pressed for travelling time. Rather it is both a crash course on Thai architectural accomplishments as well as an open-air preservation site. By recreating monuments, the museum helps to preserve traditional woodworking and construction skills that might otherwise be lost. Also the site acts as a retirement home for meritorious buildings that would otherwise be demolished.

And not only is it an ingenious way to preserve Thai architecture, it is also a thoroughly good time. You could easily spend a day here riding a bike around, waving to the Thais piled up in the back of pick-up trucks and eating at the reconstructed floating market.

En route to Muang Boran is another attraction built by the same benefactor, Prapai (Lek) Viriyahbhun, a successful business person who poured his wealth into mingling his own creativity with cultural conservation. The Erawan Museum was initially developed as a repository for Khun Lek's collection of sacred objects. Rather than follow a conventional route with a museum endowment and a bland display case, he commissioned a five-storey high sculpture of Erawan, Indra's three-headed elephant mount, to be constructed amid manicured gardens. The fanciful sculpture would represent a spiritual focal point of myth, antiquities and worship. Following the dictates of traditional stupa symbolism, the sculpture comprises three levels representing the underworld, the earth and Mount Sumeru (Hindu mythology's celestial mountain). The elephant statue is hollow inside and contains a dome-like chapel and windows overlooking the gardens. The collection of sacred antiques attracts many merit-makers, convinced that the entire site is particularly helpful in picking winning lottery numbers.

## JUST THE FACTS

Muang Boran
> Information: **Muang Boran** ( ☎ 0 2323 9253; www.ancientcity.com; KM 33, Old Th Sukhumvit; admission 300/200B; ⏰ 8am-5pm) is 33km southeast of Bangkok in the town of Samut Prakan.
> Transport: air-con bus 511 from Bangkok's Th Sukhumvit to Samut Prakan bus station (16B), then transfer to a white or red sǎwngthǎew (7B).

Erawan Museum
> Information: **Erawan Museum** ( ☎ 0 2371 3135; www.erawan-museum.com; Soi 119 Th Sukhumvit; admission 150/50B; ⏰ 8am-3pm) is 8km from Bangkok's Ekkamai bus station.
> Transport: air-con bus 511 from Bangkok's Th Sukhumvit to Samut Prakan passes by; ask for 'Chang Sam Sian' as your destination.

Eat, sleep and be merry in the City of Angels. Bangkok excels at enjoyment for roving appetites, happy-hour connoisseurs and spa aficionados. And for the culture vultures there's the rich and vibrant history of Thai Buddhism on display on household thresholds and famous temples.

Cross paths with everyone and everything on the streets of Banglamphu (p54)

SNAPSHOTS

# ACCOMMODATION

Bangkok has always known how to look after its visitors. In the days of steamer travel, the Oriental Hotel was the home-away-from-home for adventurous artists and writers, such as Somerset Maugham who spent months there recovering from a bout of malaria. During and after the Vietnam War, American soldiers R&R'd in hotels named after cities back home like Reno and Miami, while travellers on the overland hippy trail crashed at guesthouses around Soi Ngam Duphli. These days, visitors are more likely to hit the sack in the famous backpackers' ghetto of Th Khao San or live it up on a package holiday to luxury riverside hotels.

Hotels in Bangkok cover the gamut with all the attendant global trends. Most top-enders are international chains. Amenities, standards and views are phenomenal at these spots, and rates are relatively affordable compared with other metropolitan destinations worldwide. The latest trend in the upper budget range is the emergence of intimate inns reclaiming the old parts of the city where warehouses once slumbered.

The midrange options vary from superb to disturbed. Some are great value with fewer amenities than the big budget hotels but with ideal locations, while others betray Bangkok's Third World status. Beds might be a little dodgy and service a little rough around the edges.

Calls us unrepentant backpackers, but Bangkok still has the best selection of budget digs around. And the quality keeps getting better as prices climbs nominally. More and more dive hotels are being spruced up to include en suite bath, air-con and fresh coats of paint, making a little baht go a lot further.

Need a place to stay? Find and book it at lonelyplanet .com. More than 60 properties are featured for Bangkok — each personally visited, thoroughly reviewed and happily recommended by a Lonely Planet author. From hostels to high-end hotels, we've hunted out the places that will bring you unique and special experiences. Read independent reviews by authors and other travel aficionados like you, and get practical information including amenities, maps and photos. Then simply and securely book your room online. It's all at www.lonelyplanet.com/accommodation.

You've got your budget figured out, now you need to pick a neighbourhood. Most neighbourhoods are segregated into budget ranges: ie cheap guesthouses flock together in Banglamphu, while luxury hotels claim waterfront locations in the Riverside area. Another consideration is mobility. Getting around Bangkok can be a challenge, so you'll want to sleep and play in the same neighbourhood or near public transport.

Business travellers tend to stay in the white-collar districts of Silom and Sukhumvit, districts also favoured by lone male travellers for their proximity to 'entertainment' areas such as Patpong, Nana Entertainment Plaza and Soi Cowboy. Although many package deals are available for hotels in Silom and the lower-numbered *soi* of Th Sukhumvit, families or female travellers might prefer to stay in other parts of the city.

The area around Siam Square is convenient for shopaholics and is close to the Skytrain for quick trips to Sukhumvit or Silom. This is one of the most diverse budget areas, with options representing classy and homey.

The most charming place to stay is along the river, in the area we call Riverside or further north in Ko Ratanakosin or Banglamphu. In all three of these neighbourhoods, traffic can thwart an ill-timed outing. Luckily the river express ferry provides a scenic escape to many attractions. Riverside is dominated by high-end chains; Ko Ratanakosin is filling up with independent boutique inns; and Banglamphu is a gentrified backpackers' ghetto.

Devoid of pushy tailors or túk-túk drivers, Chinatown has become the 'adventurous' travellers' outpost. However, mobility is difficult due to daytime traffic.

## BEST FOR MODERN SOPHISTICATION
> Sukhothai Hotel (www.sukhothai .com)
> Peninsula Hotel (http://bangkok .peninsula.com)
> Swiss Lodge (www.swisslodge .com)

## BEST FOR COOL FACTOR
> Reflections Rooms (www.reflections -thai.com)
> Conrad Hotel (http://conradhotels1 .hilton.com)
> Seven (www.sleepatseven.com)

## BEST FOR CLASSICAL THAI
> Oriental Hotel (www.mandarinoriental .com/bangkok)
> Old Bangkok Inn (www.oldbangkokinn .com)
> Ibrik Resort (www.ibrikresort.com)
> Chakrabongse Villa (www.thaivillas.com)
> Eugenia (www.theeugenia.com)

## BEST VALUE
> Viengtai Hotel (www.viengtai.co.th)
> Royal Asia Lodge (www.royalasialodge .com)
> Baan Chantra (www.baanchantra.com)
> Ibis Siam Bangkok (www.accorhotels .com/asia)

SNAPSHOTS

# ARTS & CRAFTS

As the capital of the current dynasty, Bangkok is the nation's artistic repository, cultivating modern artists with royal patronage and preserving the art forms that were reserved solely for the royal courts. In short Bangkok is the centre of Thailand's formal arts, from temple paintings to dance-dramas. It is also the nexus of contemporary arts from graffiti to photography.

Bangkok's most impressive examples of traditional painting and sculpture are religious in nature. Temple murals painted in fantastic colours and mythological characters depict instructive sermons based on the life of Buddha or recount the *Ramakian*, the epic story adapted from India's *Ramayana*. Thai sculpture throughout its different artistic periods represent some of world's leading examples of Buddhist iconography.

Thailand began to adopt modern artistic principles in the 20th century thanks to an Italian artist named Corrado Feroci, who helped establish Silpakorn, the first fine-arts university in the kingdom. Today Thai creatives continue to capture a distinctively 'Thai' essence in modern painting and photography: religious themes are often explored through modern images and brilliant colours shape abstract scenes. In the past 10 years, the city has seen a proliferation of private galleries, mainly in the Sukhumvit and Silom area, showcasing new and established talent.

The dance-drama known as *khon* involves masked dancers depicting scenes from the *Ramakian*. Today *khon* performances are no longer cloistered in the royal courts, but are occasionally performed for the general public at the Chalermkrung Royal Theatre (p79).

Pottery and decorative arts in Thailand received much tutelage from China, but the enduring traditions of celadon (green-glazed porcelain) and *benjarong* (five-colour porcelain) retain a distinctive interplay of colours and elegance that define the Thai aesthetic. Modern interpretations of pottery and woodwork are enjoying great commercial success as is haute fashion using Thai silks and colour schemes.

Although modern Bangkok may seem like an architectural failure of soot-stained towers, the city is actually an amazing collection of traditional architecture, from the elaborate and symbolic buildings of temples and royal palaces to the residential teak homes that sheltered Thai families from the elements before the introduction of modern shophouses.

**BEST MUSEUMS & GALLERIES**
> National Museum (p47)
> Dusit Palace Park (p69)
> Chulalongkorn Art Centre (p82)
> Thailand Creative & Design Center (p124)

**BEST FOR ARCHITECTURE**
> Wat Phra Kaew (p46)
> Wat Arun (p48)
> Jim Thompson's House (p82)
> Lettuce Farm Palace (p139)
> Ban Kamthieng (p121)

# BARS & CLUBS

Bangkok is a party animal – even on a tight leash. Back in 2001, the Thaksin administration started enforcing closing times and curtailing other excesses that made Bangkok famous. Since the 2006 ouster of Thaksin, the laws have been conveniently circumvented or inconsistently enforced, and the post-coup party scene has shown signs of restoring Bangkok to its old position as Southeast Asia's fun master, a role uptight Singapore almost usurped. But it is still common for the men in brown to switch on the lights in clubs and bars way before bedtime, or at least before dawn.

During the sanctioned hours, Bangkok's watering holes range from grubby suds joints to upscale cocktail dens. A quintessential Bangkok night includes filling a plastic outdoor table with emptied bottles of beer. Th Khao San (p63) and its connected streets remain the mama-san for partying backpackers and Thai hipsters. The yuppie crowd prefers to stay chic and air-conditioned in the internationally flavoured neighbourhoods of Sukhumvit and Silom.

The club scene is equally well-versed in international trends with lounge-style venues for vinyl spinners. Be warned though, the discos burn strong and bright on certain nights – a visit from a foreign DJ or the music flavour of the month – then hibernate on other nights. Clubs geared towards foreigners usually charge a cover of about 500B, while Thais will opt for clubs with a cheaper entrance fee. Lately, RCA (Royal City Avenue) has ruled the nightscape for all ages and persuasions. Silom's gay discos on Soi 4 still pack in the sweating bodies.

The curfew has done little to curb Bangkokians' night-owl tendencies. They don't hit the clubs until midnight, pursuing *sànùk* (fun) in a shortened time-frame. Another consequence is the curiously creative methods of flouting closing times. Speakeasies have sprung up all over the city – follow the crowds, no one is heading home. Some places just remove the tables and let people drink on the floor (somehow this is an exemption), while other places serve beer in teapots. If it seems strange, welcome to Bangkok.

For more subdued tastes, Bangkok also attracts grade-A jazz musicians to several hotel bars. You'll find smokier riffs in elbow-tight rock-and-roll clubs scattered throughout the city.

Officially bars close at 1am and clubs at 2am, but this is subject to police discretion. The drinking age is 20 years old and ID checks are even enforced on grey-haired patrons.

Although Bangkok can party with global flair, let's not forget that prostitution landed it on the R&R map. Judging from the proliferation of hostess bars on Th Sukhumvit, you wouldn't think that prostitution is illegal in Thailand. Nor would you guess that most of its sex workers cater to Thais, not foreigners. But just as appearances can be deceiving, the mythology of Bangkok's sex industry – as a skin trade established by American GIs – doesn't quite match its history.

Many Thai mens' first sexual experiences are with prostitutes, considered professionals who satisfy natural male desire without compromising potential marriage partners. The homegrown industry of prostitution was finally declared illegal in the 1950s, just decades before Bangkok found its first tourist hook.

Later still Patpong (Soi Patpong 1 and 2) earned notoriety during the 1980s for its wild sex shows, involving everything from ping-pong balls to razors to midgets on motorbikes. Today it is more of a circus for curious spectators than sexual deviants. Soi Cowboy and Nana Entertainment Plaza are the real scenes of sex for hire. Not all of the love-you-long time business is geared toward Westerners: Soi Thaniya, off Th Silom, is filled with massage parlours for Japanese expats and visitors, while areas outside of central Bangkok attract Thai businessmen and police officials.

## BEST BEER BARS & COCKTAIL LOUNGES
> Wong's Place (p117)
> Cheap Charlie's (p133)
> Vino di Zanotti (p116)
> Koi (p134)
> Th Khao San (p63)
> Bamboo Bar (p107)

## BEST DANCE & MUSIC CLUBS
> Ad Here the 13th (p64)
> Bed Supperclub (p135)
> Santika (p146)
> Club Astra ((p145))
> Brown Sugar (p118)
> Saxophone (p146)

# FOOD

It's a rare moment when Bangkok residents aren't eating, planning their next meal or swapping restaurant notes. Food is everywhere, from chic eateries to streetside stalls. The city's best restaurants are glorified family kitchens where dressing to impress means wiping down the laminate tables. And almost every corner of the city boasts a small army of street vendors ranging from specialty carts to the venerable name-that-dish maestros.

The classic Bangkok eating experience is sitting on a plastic stool by the side of a traffic-choked road and eating a bowl of noodles or a simple rice dish cooked in front of you. Locals, both rich and poor, will travel any distance to their favourite stall – it's not rare to see Mercedes parked alongside motorbikes at these feeding troughs.

Once you opt for a Thai restaurant, you need to adopt a Thai frame of mind: ambience is overrated and courses are a foreign concept. Eating is a social occasion to be shared with as many people as possible. The head of the table typically orders a combination of dishes, which arrive in no particular order since they will be eaten family style. Foreigners who insist on ordering individually (and not sharing) are frequently frustrated by the kitchen's poor timing – a cross-cultural glitch, not incompetence.

While humble home-style restaurants are widespread throughout the city, finding an authentic Thai restaurant with enough ambience to qualify as a date is a tall order. Typically a beautiful setting is merely a disguise for an incompetent kitchen. When Thais celebrate a special occasion, they opt for an import cuisine, such as Italian or Chinese-style seafood, instead of their everyday menu. The thinking goes something like this: why dress up meat and three veg when you could splurge on foie gras? Exotic cuisine is relative.

Of the foreign-born meals, Italian translates well into Bangkok's steamy climate and many Italian émigrés have successfully peddled their homeland's menus to noodle loving Thais. Being a city of immigrants, Bangkok also boasts home-style restaurants from Arabia, India and China as well as various European nations to scratch an inexplicable itch for home.

**BEST HOME-STYLE THAI**
> Soi Polo Fried Chicken (p116)
> Chote Chitr (p61)
> Khrua Nopparat (p61)
> Roti-Mataba (p62)
> Pratunam Chicken Rice Restaurants (p91)

**BEST SEAFOOD RESTAURANTS**
> Ton Pho (p63)
> Soi Texas Food Stalls (p79)
> Somboon Seafood (p106)
> Ban Glang Nam (p144)

**Opposite** Let the aromas guide you for breakfast, lunch, dinner and all that's in between **Above** Thai for two

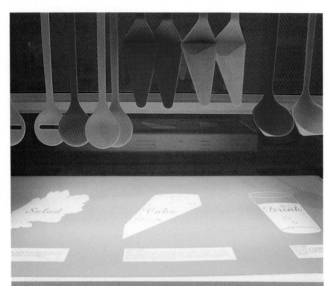

# SHOPPING & MARKETS

Even avowed anticonsumerists weaken in Bangkok. One minute they're touting the virtues of a life without material possessions, the next they're admiring the fake Rolex watches and mapping out a Skytrain route to Chatuchak Weekend Market. If you intend to launch a full-scale shopping assault, don't deny yourself a copy of the indispensable Nancy Chandler illustrated *Map of Bangkok*, widely available at local bookstores.

Let's first introduce you to Bangkok's mall culture. In some cities, frolicking outside is a common free time activity, but in Bangkok's concrete landscape and humid climate the air-conditioned malls serve as city parks. Even if their credit cards don't measure up, every able bodied Bangkokian is a de facto mall rat, strolling the halls of these consumer temples for people-watching and window shopping.

There are of course class distinctions; this is a feudal society. The socialites prefer the Emporium, the teens dig Mah Boon Krong (MBK), and everyone wanders into Siam Paragon for a photo-op in front of the ground-floor fountain. Most malls are anchored by a department store (Tokyu, Zen, Sogo etc) that gets pawed by bargain hunters during periodic sales, but the busiest part is the food court because Thais live to eat.

You'll find mainly international chains in the malls but Bangkok has a growing collection of local designer brands that combine city chic with Thai fabrics and aesthetics to produce clubwear, daywear and artwear. Even the eternally unstylish Thai politicians have spotted a trend by proclaiming Bangkok a 'Fashion City', a promotion that was ousted after the coup.

The malls, however, are just a warm-up for the markets, the cardio workout of shopping. In Bangkok, footpaths are for additional retail space not for pedestrians and where there are walkers, there are vendors. Streetside markets dominate in tourist areas, such as Th Sukhumvit, Th Silom and Th Khao San, selling everything a luggage carrier would want. Don't forget to stroll the everyday markets to see the wants and needs of Thai households.

What else can you buy in the City of Heavenly Bargains? Thanks to the diplomatic corps, Bangkok also has a sartorial tradition. As one of the world's biggest exporters of gems and ornaments, Thailand offers some good buys if you know what you're doing. Both suits and gems are prone to prolific scams so shop responsibly.

## BEST FOR FASHION & DESIGN
> Siam Square (p83)
> MBK (p85)
> Emporium (p125)
> Siam Discovery Center (p88)
> Propaganda (p88)
> Nandakwang (p127)

## BEST FOR SOUVENIRS & GIFTS
> Chatuchak Weekend Market (p143)
> Patpong Night Market (p100)
> Khao San Market (p58)
> Monk's Bowl Village (p58)
> Silom Village Trade Centre (p101)

# TEMPLES & SHRINES

Although famous for its hedonism, Bangkok is more devout than debauched. Thai Buddhism's most important figure – the king, himself – resides here as do the central temples and Buddha figures associated with the god incarnate. Below this sacred plane is the daily practice of religion, comprising local temples, famous shrines and household altars.

The older districts of Ko Ratanakosin, Thonburi and Banglamphu are the primary sightseeing spots for temple tours. Here the spires of the mosaic covered stupas are often the tallest towers in sight. There are of course the famous temples – Wat Phra Kaew, Wat Arun and Wat Pho – but to get a true sense of a temple's role in the community, visit the non-celebrities. Here you'll find clotheslines covered in the freshly laundered monk's robes, dusty yards populated by a lazy stray dog and a brood of chickens, and Thai matrons in their finest silks making merit. In the early mornings, the novice monks traverse the neighbourhoods in bare feet collecting alms for their day's meal.

Religious devotion is not confined to the whitewashed temple walls. In Bangkok, sacred spaces are as prolific as traffic jams. Thailand's version of Buddhism is heavily spiced with animistic spirit worship. These spirits dwell in earthly spaces and are often given their own residences, in the case of the spirit houses and shrines occupying homes or business. Spirits that tinker with fate and fortune are often appeased with daily offerings of food and drink set out upon a doorstep or a dedicated altar within the home.

Even the body is transformed into a walking altar – most Thais wear amulets to protect them from harm and ensure good fortune. For taxi and bus drivers, their vehicles become a moving temple displaying stickers of famous monks and flower garland offerings. Treating the unknown forces of fate with respect might appear more important than obeying traffic rules.

Chinatown provides an interesting counterpoint to Thai Buddhism. Ancestor worship plays a larger role in Chinese Buddhism and morning rituals often include the burning of paper offerings to the deceased in streetside bins.

## BEST TEMPLES & SHRINES
> Wat Pho (p50)
> Wat Phra Kaew (p46)
> Wat Arun (p48)
> Trok Itsaranuphap (p75)
> Amulet Market (p50)
> Erawan Shrine (p82)
> Wat Saket & Golden Mount (p57)

## BEST SPOTS TO STUDY MEDITATION
> World Fellowship of Buddhists (p137)
> Dhamma Talk: Vipassana Meditation Section (p53)
> House of Dhamma (p145)

**Opposite** The longest reclining Buddha in the land at Wat Pho (p50) **Above** Temple guardians, Wat Phra Kaew (p46)

# THAI COOKING COURSES

Why let a plump tummy be the only sign of a visit to Thailand? Instead, learn to create the kingdom's zesty dishes in your own kitchen to counter a ho-hum menu or spice up a dinner party.

Cooking schools in Bangkok range from formal affairs for amateur chefs to home-cooking for the recipe-phobic. Everyone always has a grand time, fumbling with ingredients, tasting the fruits of their labour and trotting home with new cooking techniques. Classes are usually held twice a day (one in the morning and one in the afternoon). In the instructional kitchens, students prepare about five dishes, ranging from simple to complex, and classes may also include a takeaway recipe book. Preparing some of Thailand's most famous dishes provides a greater appreciation of the interplay of flavours and inherent artistry. The ingredients of a dish should have eye-pleasing colours as well as mouth-pleasing flavours. You'll soon discover that a well-kept secret of Thai cuisine is that most dishes are made up of the same humble ingredients although the end result is surprisingly diverse.

Some classes also offer market tours that explain the various ingredients on sale and offer a glimpse into the shopping habits of Thai housewives. Knowing your way around a food market is essential for attaining Thai 'foodie' status. Day markets are divided into two sections: fresh produce on one side, freshly butchered meat and fish on the 'wet' side (so named because this area is hosed down at the close of business). You'll be amazed by the collage of fruits, vegetables and herbs that Thailand's fecund climate produces.

Market shopping is a social affair in Bangkok, with vendors sweet-talking passing customers or gossiping among themselves. It is also a pantry exploration, where you can inspect the conical mounds of prepared curry paste, stacks of aromatic herbs and tables full of exotic fruits. After picking up the day's supplies, market-shoppers usually refuel with a plate of *khànǒm jiin* (stark white rice noodles served with curries)

### BEST COOKING COURSES
> Oriental Hotel Cooking Centre (p110)
> Blue Elephant Cooking School (p109)
> Manohra Cruises Cooking Courses (p146)
> Silom Thai Cooking School (p111)
> Epicurean Kitchen (p109)

### BEST SPOTS FOR COOKING SUPPLIES
> Chatuchak Weekend Market (p143)
> Nittaya Curry Shop (p58)
> Soi Pradit (Soi 20) Market (p105)

# BANGKOK FOR KIDS

Most big cities act like your bachelor buddies toward kids – awkward and slightly annoyed. But Bangkok has a grandmother's appreciation of little ones, transforming a fairly self-absorbed city into cooing admirers. Thais are especially tickled by fat-cheeked babies and often describe them as 'pinchable', a term of affection. But children of all ages will find a warm reception in Bangkok. Hotel staff might shower them with sweets and adults will yield a seat on public transport to kids.

The kid attractions in Bangkok don't get as much press as the adult options, but there is plenty to keep them engaged and entertained. Despite your best efforts, your children's favourite activity will probably be the hotel pool. Many are tropically landscaped, have views of the city and fewer rules than back home. Older children will find the markets and shopping malls to be their new best friends. There are also kid-targeted spots: Dusit Zoo and the Children's Museum, which get mixed reviews.

Don't rule out excursions that you would like for the sake of your kids. Many parents have reported that canal tours were a real hit as were strolls through wet markets to check out all the strange critters for sale (buckets of eels, slimy frogs and flapping fish).

Between February and April, Bangkok's parks host kite fights, which pit different teams flying either a 'male' or 'female' kite against each other. The teams are assigned a particular territory, winning points if they can force a competitor into their zone.

## BEST KID-FRIENDLY PLAY SPOTS
> Krung Sri IMAX (p92)
> SF City Bowl (p93)
> Baiyoke Sky Tower (p139)
> Plan Creations (p101)
> Wat Prayoon (p50)

## BEST KID-FRIENDLY MUSEUMS & ATTRACTION'S
> Bangkok Doll Factory & Museum (p139)
> Siam Ocean World (p83)
> Children's Discovery Museum (p139)
> Museum of Forensic Medicine (p47)
> Queen Saovabha Memorial Institute Snake Farm (p96)

# GAY & LESBIAN BANGKOK

In anything-goes Bangkok, gays and lesbians enjoy an unprecedented amount of acceptance considering the conservative views of the region. Gay professionals enjoy relative equality in the workplace and a pride parade is celebrated annually with great fanfare. Homosexual couples, as well as straight couples, do not show public affection, unless they are purposefully flouting social mores.

A long-standing social phenomenon in Thailand is the third gender (*kàthoey*), often translated into English as 'lady boy'. Some are cross-dressers, while others have had sexual reassignment surgery. (Thailand is one of the leading countries for this procedure.) Regardless of their anatomy, most *kàthoey* assume an exaggerated feminine persona, often wearing more make-up than Thai women. Foreigners are especially fascinated by lady-boys as they are often very convincing women, and *kàthoey* cabarets aimed at tourists are popular venues for observing gender bending.

In terms of nightlife, Bangkok has a well-defined pink triangle around Th Silom. Dead-end Soi 2 is packed with pretty-boy discos, while Soi 4 has the people-watching bars. Th Sarasin's bars are little more local and low-key. There is also a local Thai scene in Chatuchak.

Bangkok used to ignore lesbians (known locally as *tom-dee*), but that has changed with the emergence of women-only clubs in the Lumphini and RCA areas. For more leads on Bangkok's gay scene, check out Utopia (www.utopia-asia.com), which lists Bangkok events and goings-on, and Gyent (www.gyent.com), which organises theme parties at various venues.

## BEST ....
> For meeting the locals – ICY (p145)
> For people-watching – Balcony Bar (p107) and Telephone (p108)
> For sweating to techno – DJ Station (p109)
> For lady-boy cabaret – Freeman (p110)
> For a buffet of bars – Th Sarasin Bars (p117)
> For the girls – Zeta (p148)

V

SNAPSHOTS

# PARKS & GARDENS

Some Bangkok residents confess to the odd fantasy of rolling on a patch of lawn, such is the pitiful amount of park space in the city. But the green that grows in the city sprouts all sorts of activity in the cooler hours of the day. Parks support daily aerobics classes, family gatherings and even the pick-up past-time of *tàkrâw*, an old Siamese game of keeping a rattan ball airborne with the feet. Like *muay thai* (Thai boxing), the art is in the kick with points awarded for style, difficulty and variety. There is always a corner of a park filled with food vendors serving snacks and drinks to off-set dehydration and calorie burning.

More dynamic than the city parks are various common spaces between commercial districts. The elevated walkways outside certain Skytrain stations are used for modern-day promenading. Breakdancers show off their spins and dance steps, couples stroll hand-in-hand and bootleg vendors sell their wares in between police rounds. Below these pedestrian-only places are Bangkok's swollen rivers of traffic.

Even the shopping malls are treated more like parks than enterprise. On weekends, the central foyers of everyman-friendly malls are filled with teenagers sucking down petite ice-cream cones or grandmas nervously stepping onto the escalators. The stores might be quiet but the hallways hum with socialising.

**BEST PEOPLE-WATCHING PLACES**
> National Stadium (Map p81, A2) and Victory Monument (Map p140—1, C5) Skytrain stations
> Ground floor atrium of Siam Paragon (p89)
> Soi 7 of Siam Square (p89)
> MBK (p85)

**BEST GREEN ZONES**
> Lumphini Park (p114)
> Santichaiprakan Park (p56)
> Benjasiri Park (p121)
> Chuvit Garden (p121)

# SPAS & WELLNESS CENTRES

This city aims to please. Add in a tradition of massage and a favour-able currency exchange rate and you've got yourself a spa date. Spa treatments that might cost a small fortune in any other metropolis are thankfully discounted in the City of Angelic Prices. Bangkok's day spas are also up to speed on all of the international techniques: you can be kneaded like dough, bathed in mud, dunked in flowers and wrapped in seaweed. Tony Chi's minimalist spa designs enjoy a Bangkok address as do traditional Thai-style homes transformed into a garden of tranquil-lity. You can do a full-on spa cottage, with in-room treatments, or just a couple's package overlooking the Bangkok skyline. More down market are the little storefronts that will pluck and wax errant hairs, sculpt talons into nails and tint away hints of grey. Beauty runs a close second behind food as a citywide obsession.

If you need more than an image upgrade, Bangkok can oblige as well. Medical tourism, an apparent oxymoron, is a booming business here. Bangkok's hospitals are on par with top-tier Western facilities and cover all the bases – including dentistry, nips and tucks, corrective and elective surgeries – for less than the price at home. Some folks mix medical with pleasure by scheduling a procedure they couldn't afford at home with a recuperative stay at a nearby beach resort.

More recently, wellness centres have begun to offer a combination of Western and alternative therapies to address weight problems and substance addiction.

## BEST...
> For jet lag massage – Oriental Spa Thai Health & Beauty Centre (p111)
> For honeymoon couples – Banyan Tree Spa (p117)
> For spa cottages – Baan Thai Wellness Retreat (p134)
> For Thai elegance – DVN Spa & Wellbeing Center (p135)
> For health treatments – Rasayana Retreat (p136)
> For quick and cheap facials – Angela Beauty Care (p65)
> For intimate day spa – Spa 1930 (p93)

# TRADITIONAL MASSAGE

Once you've been stretched, pulled, kneaded and pinched, you'll realise why a Thai massage isn't the luxurious indulgence you might expect. Thailand's interpretation is a combination of yoga and acupressure resulting in a passive workout. Although a foot in your armpit might not be your idea of relaxation, these lever-like positions are time-tested for unclogging energy meridians and promoting health. Devotees describe a comfortable euphoria setting in after a particularly forceful session and some even use massage to treat chronic pain and disease. In fact, massage is considered a vital component to overall health as necessary as diet and exercise.

There is no shortage of massage shops in Bangkok, but not all are created equally. Some blur the line between ancient massage and 'recreation' (often providing happy endings for male patrons), while others are massage assembly-lines with a constant stream of prostrate bodies. For men who wish to avoid a massage surprise, look for a parlour employing old ladies rather than pretty young things.

There is also a huge menu of massage styles: foot, full body and full body with oil or herbal compresses. Although the masseuses might seem demure, their fingers are like steel vices that can manipulate brawny patrons into puddles of jelly. Any massage is good, but finding a great massage depends on matching your personal threshold for pain with the masseuse's grip. No pain, no gain is the mantra of some, while others prefer to be pummelled more tenderly. Most, however, will agree that a massage a day will keep the doctor (or at least the aches) away.

## BEST...
> For foot massages – Buathip Thai Massage (p135)
> For studying Thai massage – Wat Pho Massage School (p53)
> For post-shopping massage – Thann Sanctuary (p93)
> For treating generic aches – Healthland Spa & Massage (p110)
> For a traditional Thai setting – Ruen-Nuad Massage (p111)

A simple river cruise reveals some awe-inspiring sights, such as Wat Pho (p50)

# BACKGROUND
## HISTORY
### A SIAMESE CAPITAL

Bangkok is the phoenix-risen of the Thai kingdom, the second chance after the nation's thriving capital, Ayuthaya, was devastated by Burmese invaders in 1767. In the ensuing collapse, General Taksin emerged as the primary leader, forcing out the Burmese and establishing a new capital in Thonburi, on the western bank of Mae Nam Chao Phraya. Taksin's reunification of the country was decisive, but his ruling style was ruthless. By 1782, Chao Phraya Chakri, a key general, deposed Taksin as king and moved the capital across the river to modern-day Bangkok. Chakri's son inherited the throne, thus establishing the Chakri dynasty, which is still in place today.

Rama I (Chao Phraya Chakri) chose the eastern bank of the river as a defensive measure against possible Burmese invasions. Canals *(khlong)* were dug to replicate the island-city of Ayuthaya and artisans were commissioned to build great temples to replace those destroyed in the old capital. The waterways were a key element in the cycle of life.

Reforms during the mid-18th and early 19th centuries – enacted by Rama IV (King Mongkut; r 1851–68) and his son, Rama V (King Chulalongkorn; r 1868–1910) – took the country into the modern era. Changes included the creation of a civil service, still one of Bangkok's biggest employers, eradication of slavery and successful defence of Thailand's independence during European colonisation.

You'd never know it today, but Bangkok's first road (Th Charoen Krung, also known as the 'New Rd') wasn't built until the 1860s. As motorised transport took off, Bangkok expanded in every direction, often building over former canals.

The political landscape changed rapidly, too, with a bloodless coup in 1932 abruptly ending the era of absolute monarchy and ushering in a constitutional monarchy. Then in 1939 the country's official name changed from Siam to Thailand. Bangkok's infamous sex industry expanded during the Vietnam War, when it was a popular R&R stop for foreign troops.

In the 1970s, democracy was on a shaky path – the military brutally suppressed a pro-democracy student rally in Bangkok and the country later see-sawed between civilian and military rule. Big demonstrations in 1992, calling for the resignation of the latest military dictator, saw violent street confrontations near Democracy Monument, resulting in 50 civilian deaths. After a right royal scolding from the king, the dictator resigned. Since 1992, the country has been ruled by democratically elected civilian coalitions.

## BANGKOK TODAY

In the last decades of the 20th century, Bangkok was the beating heart of one of Asia's hottest economies. Modern skyscrapers tickled the skyline, and the middle and upper classes flaunted Western luxury goods. But in 1997, the bubble burst and the Thai currency spiralled ever downwards. By the new millennium, the Thai economy was back on track showing more sustainable growth than in the boom-and-bust years. The city continued to mature by developing two public transit systems: the BTS Skytrain and MRTA Metro Subway, both civic-minded novelties to the traffic-choked city. Campaigns to 'clean up the city' – be it crackdowns on police corruption or early closing times for bars – were spearheaded by former prime minister Thaksin Shinawatra.

The 1997 passage of a national constitution ensured more human and civil rights and was supposed to signal Thailand's successful coming-of-age as a democracy. It was abolished in 2006 during the country's most recent coup to unseat then prime minister Thaksin Shinawatra, a telecommunications billionaire, and his Thai Rak Thai (Thais Love Thais) Party. Thaksin had swept into power in 2001 on a populist platform widely supported by rural voters. By 2005 his party had won a larger majority of the National Assembly, effectively creating one-party rule in the kingdom. Bangkok's intellectuals were miffed as Thaksin used his power to suppress media freedoms, pass legislation that favoured his and his cronies commercial ventures and punish the city for electing the opposition party in 2006 municipal elections.

In 2006 Bangkok street protests against Thaksin's alleged abuses of power resulted in his dissolution of the parliament and calling of a snap election to secure his popular mandate. The election was boycotted by the opposition party and the results were later nullified by the constitutional court, who ordered a new round of elections for the National Assembly to be held in October 2006. In the meantime Thaksin still retains control of the provisional government but his role in the political future is uncertain.

**TONGUE-TWISTING TITLE**

At 26 words long, Bangkok's Thai name is a bit of a mouthful, so everyone shortens it to 'Krung Thep', or 'City of Angels'. The full-length version can be translated as: 'Great city of angels, the repository of divine gems, the great land unconquerable, the grand and prominent realm, the royal and delightful capital full of nine noble gems, the highest royal dwelling and grand palace, the divine shelter and living place of reincarnated spirits'. Foreigners, however, never bothered to learn either and continued to call the capital 'Bang Makok' (Village of Olive Plums), which was eventually truncated to 'Bangkok'.

Usually Thai politics is stuffy and unintelligible, but political theatre dominated 2006 and 2007. Bangkok street protesters (an unusual sight in itself) rang in the new year of 2006 calling for Thaksin's resignation over the tax-free sale of his family's telecommunications business (Shin Corporation) as well as suspicions that he had ambitions to assume the throne from the current and ageing king. Thaksin challenged his critics by dissolving parliament and calling for new elections that would prove his popular mandate. Before legitimate elections were held, military tanks rolled into Bangkok and told Thaksin, who was in New York at the time, not to come back. The city initially rejoiced after its 'liberation' from the democratically elected tyrant and coup leaders promised speedy elections with a new and improved constitution. But by early 2007 a smooth restoration of democracy looked unlikely. The New Year's Eve bombings, which targeted high-profile festivities in Bangkok, and the government's botched attempts at currency regula-tion spooked foreign investment in the country and cast doubts on the success of post-Thaksin Thailand.

# LIFE AS A BANGKOK RESIDENT
## CITY OF ANGELS

Bangkok is both utterly Thai and totally foreign. Old and new ways clash and mingle, constantly redrawing the lines of what it means to be 'Thai'. The city has a huge concentration of citizens with disposable income, from the empire princesses of the hi-so (high society) scene to the teenagers hanging out in Siam Square. In certain circles, Bangkok will seem decidedly westernised with bilingual, foreign-educated Thais more familiar with the *Simpsons* than squat toilets. But despite the international veneer, a Thai value system – built primarily on religious and monarchical devotion – is ticking away, guiding every aspect of life. Almost all Thais, even the most conspicuously consuming, are dedicated Buddhists who aim to be reborn into a better life by making merit (giving donations to temples or feeding monks), regarding merit-making as the key to their earthly success.

Bangkok accommodates every rung of the economic ladder, from the aristocrat to the slum dweller. It is the new start for the economic hopefuls and the last chance for the economic refugees. The lucky ones from the bottom rung form the working class backbone of the city – taxi drivers, food vendors, maids, nannies and even prostitutes. Many hail from the northeastern provinces and send hard-earned baht back to their families in small rural villages. At the very bottom are the disposed, who live in squatter communities on marginal, often polluted land. While the Thai economy has surged, a social net has yet to be constructed. Meanwhile, Bangkok is also the great incubator for Thailand's new generation of young creatives, from designers to architects, and has long nurtured the archetype of the country's middle class.

The city has also represented economic opportunity for foreign immigrants. Approximately a quarter of the city's population claims some Chinese ancestry, be it Cantonese, Hainanese, Hokkien or Teochew. Although the first Chinese labourers faced discrimination from the Thais, their descendants' success in business, finance and public affairs helped to elevate the status of Chinese and Thai-Chinese families. In fact, many of the ruling mercantile families are Thai-Chinese and even the present king has some Chinese heritage.

Immigrants from South Asia also migrated to Bangkok and comprise the second-largest Asian minority. Sikhs from northern India typically make their living in tailoring, while Sinhalese, Bangladeshis, Nepalis and Pakistanis can be found in the import-export or retail trade.

## DID YOU KNOW?

> Women constitute half of the workforce in Bangkok.
> Bangkok's minimum daily wage is 181B (US$4.52).
> Bangkok was recently rated the world's hottest city (in terms of temperature) by the World Meteorological Organization.
> Rama IX is the world's longest-reigning monarch.

## MONARCHY

The Thais relationship with their king is deeply spiritual and intensely personal. Many view him as a god (all Thai kings are referred to as 'Rama', one of the incarnations of the Hindu god Vishnu) and as a father figure (the king's birthday is the national celebration of Father's Day). The reigning monarch, King Bhumibol Adulyadej, inherited automatic reverence when he assumed the throne, but he captured the Thai people's hearts with his actions. When he was younger, he was fashion-able and photogenic: scooting around town in a yellow Rolls Royce (yellow is the colour associated with the day of the week the king was born) and playing jazz saxophone. He embodied the ideal modern Thai, cultured and cosmopolitan yet respectful of tradition. His role as a figurehead of the nation was augmented with his role as a provider and protector through well-publicised projects aimed at the country's struggling farmers.

Pictures of the king and the queen line the royal avenue of Th Ratchad-amnoen and many Thais will *wâi* the pictures as they pass on their daily commute. Drivers also decorate their cars with bumper stickers that read: 'We Love the King'.

In June 2006, the king celebrated his 60th year on the throne, an event regarded by many Thais as bittersweet because the ageing king (now 80 years old) may soon leave the helm of the Thai nation. His son, Crown Prince Maha Vajiralongkorn, has been chosen to succeed him, but it is the king's daughter Princess Mahachakri Sirindhorn that many Thais feel a deeper connection with because she has followed in her father's philanthropic footsteps.

## ETIQUETTE

Just remember to respect two things: religion and the monarchy. This means standing when the national or royal anthem is played (before movies and at 8am and 6pm daily); not criticising the king or his family; and dressing respectfully at royal buildings and temples (with shoulders and legs covered, and shoes removed before entering buildings). Keep your feet pointed away from a Buddha image. Monks aren't supposed to touch or be touched by women.

Other ways to avoid offending Thais include: not wearing shoes inside people's homes; not touching anyone's head; and keeping your feet and shoes on the floor, not on a chair or table. Remember to keep your cool

## WHEN TO WÂI
Elegant and complicated, the traditional Thai greeting is the *wâi*, a gesture where palms are put together, prayerlike. The placement of the hands in relation to the face is a delicate formula, dependent on the status of the two people *wâi*-ing each other. Thais don't expect foreigners to understand this rule, but it is polite to return a *wâi* to a friend, co-worker and definitely to a VIP. The biggest mistake made by foreigners is to throw out a *wâi* to every door attendant. When you are the customer, you don't *wâi* the server – that means the noodle vendor, tailor and concierge, even if you're really happy.

as getting angry or talking loudly is thought rude. Losing your temper is considered a major loss of face for both parties. The better approach is to speak softly and smile – Thais are suckers for a good smile.

Pedestrian behaviour in Bangkok can be off-putting for Westerners accustomed to more orderly street etiquette. Remember that pedestrians have no rights when interacting with cars, motorcycles or even push-carts. When crossing a street stalled with traffic, look between the lanes for speeding motorcycles.

# ART & ARCHITECTURE
Both a modern metropolis and a traditional village, Bangkok provides a glimpse into the artistic treasures of the Thai kingdom.

## TEMPLES & TOWERS
Sitting in the river delta of the central plains, Bangkok was built beside the river or canals by a people who knew how to cope with the monsoon rains and seasonal flooding. Traditional teak homes were built on stilts, either single-room houses or houses interconnected by walkways. Roof-lines were steep and often decorated with spiritual motifs. The functional elements of traditional construction protected the homes from water-ways that jumped their banks during the rainy season. And when the water dried up and the sun beat down, the undercarriage of the homes provided a shady and breezy escape.

In the realm of cultural artisanship, Thailand's energies were chan-nelled into temple (wat) architecture. Of the core components of a tem-ple complex, the *chedi* (stupa, where holy relics are stored) is a poignant example of outside influences in early Thai history. A bell-shaped *chedi* is often credited to the style of Ceylon (Sri Lanka), which participated with Thailand in many monastic exchanges, and the corn-cob-shaped *prang* is an inheritance from the Khmer empire. The dazzling colours and sparkling mosaics are all Thai.

Around the 19th century, Bangkok adopted the Sino-Portuguese–style shophouses and warehouses that lined the waterways of neighbouring port cities such as Singapore and Penang. Traditional elements were mixed with these neoclassical trends and dubbed Ratanakosin, (or old Bangkok) style. The old ministry buildings in Ko Ratanakosin are leading examples. Later, Thai techniques merged with Victorian sentiments in the feminine confection of buildings at Dusit Palace Park (p18).

The city started growing skyward in the 1970s. First slowly with the Dusit Thani Hotel on Th Silom, which climbed higher than the city's temple spires, and then in a mad rush during the close of the millennium. By the year 2000, nearly a thousand buildings could claim the same distinction, with at least 20 of them towering higher than 45 floors. The most flamboyant of the late 1980s is the former headquarters of the Bank of Asia, better known as the Robot Building, on Th Sathon Tai. The building's façade is decorated with industrial components, suggesting a super-sized robot. If you get enough altitude on the city, you'll also spot a building with the silhouette of an elephant. The towers that followed this playful period are more subdued geometric structures. The tallest scraper in the Bangkok (and the country's) skyline is the Baiyoke Sky Hotel, which is unfortunately dwarfed in the region by Kuala Lumpur's Petronas Twin Towers. Ever optimistic and slightly superficial, Bangkok developers have plans to puncture the sky with the world's tallest building, a blueprint that may never progress past one dimension.

## VISUAL ARTS

Thailand's most famous contributions to the world of art has been Buddha sculptures. Traditional Thai painting was limited to intricate representations of *Ramakian* and *Jataka,* tales of the Buddha's past lives, painted as sermons on temple walls.

Italian artist Corrado Feroci is often credited for jump-starting Thailand's secular art movement. He designed the Democracy Monument and developed the first fine arts department, now at Silpakorn University. Bangkok continues to foster Thailand's avant-garde. Internationally known Montien Boonma uses abstract symbolism to revisit traditional

Buddhist themes. Reactionary artists, such as Manit Sriwanichpoom, often mix pop aesthetics with social commentary. Thaweesak Srithong-dee's cheeky superheroes and sculptor Manop Suwanpinta's human anatomy pieces are confoundingly meaningless yet profound.

## THEATRE & DANCE

The stage in Thailand typically hosts a *khon* performance, one of the six traditional dramatic forms. It's extravagant and a visual feast, where hundreds of characters love and die, fight and dance. Acted only by men, *khon* drama is based upon stories of the *Ramakian*, Thailand's version of India's epic *Ramayana*, and was traditionally only for royal audiences.

The less formal *lákhon* dances, of which there are many dying sub-genres, usually involve costumed dancers (of both sexes) performing elements of the *Ramakian* and traditional folk tales. The most widespread variation is called *lákhon kâe bon,* which is commissioned by worshippers at shrines to earn merit.

Royal marionettes *(lákhon lék),* once on the brink of extinction, have been revived by Joe Louis Puppet Theatre (p118). The metre-high creations are elaborately costumed and perform all the subtle manipulations required of their human *khon* counterparts.

## MUSIC

The traditional Thai orchestra *(pìiphâat)* is made up of the rhythmic clinking of cymbals, the whine of the stringed *saw* and the playful rain sounds of the *ránâat èhk* (wooden xylophone), along with another five to 20 instruments. The snake-charmer sounds of the *pìi* (oboe-like woodwind) usually accompanies Thai-boxing matches.

Modern Thai music ranges from sappy pop tunes and heartbreaking ballads to protest songs. Taxi drivers love the *lûuk thûng* (literally 'children of the fields') music genre, from the rural northeastern provinces. There's a definite croon feel to it, though the subject matter mines the faithful country-and-western themes of losing your job, your wife and your buffalo. Rock bands Carabao and Caravan have earned legendary status for their politically charged songs, termed *phleng phêua chii-wít* (songs for life).

Today the alternative hordes are celebrating the amorphic genre of indie, including everything from alt-rock, rap and ska-funk recorded on

**BKK HITLIST**

Need to know who's who in Bangkok's musical soundscape? Poets, punks and pop stars get top billing.

> *That Song* (Modern Dog) Thailand's grunge gurus' latest album containing the hit song 'Dta Sawang' (Clear Eyes).
> *Made in Thailand* (Carabao) The classic Thai rock album. Check out the eponymous song's English chorus.
> *Khon Kap Khwai* (Caravan) Considered one of the first albums of *phleng phêua chii-wít*
> *Best* (Pumpuang Duanjan) A collection of songs from *lûuk thûng*'s diva.
> *I Believe* (Tata Young) Thailand's pop goddess won international fans with this English-language album, full of snappy tweener hits.
> *Best of Loso* (Loso) — An introduction to the songs that most Thais can sing by heart.

independent labels. Tune into the radio station 104.5 FM Fat Radio or catch weekend shows at Centrepoint Plaza (Siam Square Soi 7 between Soi 3 & 4) or Th Khao San for the latest Thai indie music.

# GOVERNMENT & POLITICS

Bangkok is the seat of the national government, based on the British system of constitutional monarchy. Or at least it was a constitutional monarchy until the 2006 military coup dissolved the constitution and the parliament. An interim civilian government was appointed and made promises made that a new constitution and elections would follow shortly. What has seemed like just another Thai coup – there have been 18 during the country's modern history – has taken an uncertain turn. At the time of research, experts were unsure if and when democracy will be restored, and if the military junta will ultimately succeed in undoing Thaksin's popular support, influence in exile and personal empire.

The city is administered by a popularly elected governor and is divided into 50 districts (called *khet*) and 154 subdistricts (called *kwaeng*). Bangkok is typically more liberal than the rest of the country, but clear political distinctions exist between the working class and the elite. The 2004 win of the Bangkok gubernatorial election by Democrat Apirak Kosayodhin was widely regarded as a protest vote by the citizens of the capital against the authoritarian style of then prime minister Thaksin Shinawatra and his populist Thai Rak Thai party. In the 2006 district elections, Democrats won additional support, garnering 61% of the seats. Governor Apirak's city administration has been involved in several corruption scandals regarding city contracts. Until the ouster of the Thaksin administration in 2006, the Democratic municipal government and the Thai Rak Thai national government stalemated over the extension of Bangkok's public transportation network. The proposed extensions received renewed momentum affter the 2006 military coup.

# ENVIRONMENT

We won't lie to you – Bangkok is polluted. The combination of tropical heat and air pollution will leave you covered in sweat and gasping for fresh air. The air quality becomes most stultifying at major intersections, with asphyxiating vehicle emissions and particulate matter. Over the past 10 years, Bangkok has eradicated much of the most toxic elements of air pollution – lead and sulphur dioxide – but still struggles with dangerous levels of particulate matter created by automobiles and construction projects.

Bangkok is also a damned noisy place round the clock, as you'll discover if you stay near a construction site jumping with jackhammers. Screaming motorcycles and thundering buses also comprise the Bangkok symphony that often blots out streetside conversations.

There has been an effort to clean up the waterways over recent decades. The results are most noticeable in the river, still used daily by residents for bathing, laundry and drinking water (after treatment). The canals on the Bangkok side are particularly murky and are still used as garbage disposals. When riding the *khlong* taxi, locals cover their faces with handkerchiefs or crouch behind the adjustable plastic tarp when the boat hits an errant wave.

# FURTHER READING & FILMS

Much of the literature that shapes Bangkok's modern psyche has not been translated into English. One of the few exceptions set in Bangkok is *Married to the Demon King*, translated and notated by Susan Fulop Kepner and based on Sri Daoruang's tale of a modern-day Bangkok marriage drawing from the epic characters of the *Ramakian*.

Most Thais are avid comic book readers but rarely commit themselves to publications with more meat. The city's bookstores are also well stocked with art and design magazines, catering to the recent obsession with style and commercial design.

In addition to the many books that decipher Thai culture for Western readers, *Very Thai: Everyday Pop Culture*, by Philip Cornwel-Smith, explains in a series of essays, Bangkok's many oddities from taxi shrines to the city's obsession with uniforms. *Bangkok*, by William Warren, isn't so much a cultural exploration as an historical memoir and tribute to the city. *Vanishing Bangkok*, a photo-essay by Surat Osathanugrah, documents the activities in and around the city's disappearing canals.

In the novel department, most English-language books about Bangkok are dominated by formulaic sex-capades, dealing mainly with brothels and gangsters. The most insightful is the hard-boiled crime thriller *Bangkok 8,* by John Burdett, whose hero is a collection of opposites: a Thai *faràng* cop who grew up in the brothels but matured in the monastery. *Jasmine Nights*, by SP Somtow, follows the coming-of-age of an upper-middle class Bangkok teenager. *Sightseeing*, by Rattawut Lapcharoensap, is a collection of short stories about functional and dysfunctional families in Bangkok.

When it comes to Thai cinema, there are some exceptional stories that poignantly capture Bangkok and then there's lots of mediocre fluff that requires a deep appreciation of Thailand rather than good cinema. You are usually in good hands with any film made by Pen-Ek Ratanaruang, the county's leading alt-film director. His debut film was *Fun Bar Karaoke*, a 1997 satire of Bangkok life in which the main characters are an ageing Thai playboy and his daughter. *Mon Rak Transistor* (2001) spins the tragicomic odyssey of a young villager who tries to crack the big time *lûuk thûng* music scene in Bangkok. But it will be the atmospheric tale of *Ruang Rak Noi Nid Mahasan* (*Last Life in the Universe;* 2003), written by Prabda Yoon, that will secure Pen-Ek's work a position in cinema classics.

# DIRECTORY
## TRANSPORT
### ARRIVAL & DEPARTURE
Bangkok is a major travel hub for the region, and with the upcoming completion of the Suvanabhumi airport, capacity will increase. No frills, low cost airlines have also sprouted for short hops within Thailand and the region. Bus and train services are comfortable and affordable, albeit slower.

### AIR
Bangkok's new international airport (known as Suvanabhumi) has already opened, but the old Don Mueang airport was brought out of retirement to handle certain domestic flights. Check with the ticketing agent or airline about which airport your domestic flights will be using to avoid confusion.

### Suvanabhumi (Bangkok International) Airport
Located 25km east of the city, Suvanabhumi (pronounced soo-vana-poom) airport opened in 2006 to much national pride and fanfare. The grand plans for the new airport included it being the largest airport in Southeast Asia and becoming the regional hub. Some six months later, construction flaws and safety concerns scarred the airport's optimistic beginnings.

Despite the airport's shortcomings, as of writing, all international flights are still scheduled for arrival and departure from here. For general inquiries, contact ☎ 0 2723 0000 or www .bangkokairportonline.com.

**Airport Access**
The airport is accessible by highway links, and estimated transit time to central Bangkok is 35 to 45 minutes.

The public transportation centre is 3km from the airport terminal and includes a public bus terminal, metered taxi stand, car rental and long-term parking. An airport shuttle running both an ordinary and express route connects the transportation centre with the passenger terminals.

Metered taxis are available curbside from the airport terminals and from the taxi stand at the public transportation centre. Typical metered fares from the airport are as follows: 200B to 250B to Th Sukhumvit, 250B to 300B to Th Khao San, 500B to Mo Chit. Toll charges (paid by the passenger) vary between 20B to 60B. Do note that there is also a 50B surcharge that is added to all fares departing from the airport payable to the driver.

You can hail a taxi directly from the street for airport trips or you can arrange one through the hotels or by calling ☎ 1681 (which charges a 20B dispatch surcharge).

Airport express buses operate along four routes between central Bangkok and the airport between 5am to midnight. The cost is 150B. Route AE1 travels to Silom, AE2 to Banglamphu/Th Khao San, AE3 to Th Sukhumvit and Th Withayu (Wireless Rd) and AE4 to Hualamphong train station.

Public buses serving the airport's transportation centre include six Bangkok routes and three provincial routes. Buses to Bangkok travel to the following destinations and cost around 35B: Minburi (549), Happy Land (550), Victory Monument (551), On Nut Skytrain station (552), Samut Prakan (553) and Don Mueang (554). From these points, you can continue on public transport or taxi to your hotel. If your hotel is in Banglamphu, the Victory Monument bus will be the closest option; for Siam Square, Sukhumvit or Silom, use the On Nut bus.

At that time of research, the Airport Train Link was tentatively scheduled for completion in 2008. This will provide a service from the airport to central Bangkok at Makkasan (corner Th Phetburi and Th Ratchadaphisek,

with access to Phetburi subway station) and Phayathai (corner of Th Phayathai and Phra Ram VI, with access to the Phayathai Skytrain station). According to initial planning, the express train service will take about 15 minutes to reach the airport. The line will also be used for commuter services with stops at eight stations between the airport and the central terminus. The airport train link began with great gusto two years ago but has since lagged behind the progress of the new airport making the 2008 opening date an optimistic one.

### Don Mueang Airport (formerly Bangkok International Airport)

Don Mueang Airport, 25km north of Bangkok, was officially retired from commercial service in September 2006 but was resurrected at the beginning of 2007 to handle overflow traffic from the troubled Suvanabhumi airport. As of writing, the following domestic carriers were operating out of Don Mueang: Thai Airways (domestic flights only), Nok Air and One-Two-Go. Be sure to monitor Don Mueang's status prior to your trip as it was unclear if the old airport's role would be temporary, limited to certain carriers or expanded to include all domestic service.

For general Inquiries and flight Information, contact ☎ 0 2535 1111 or www.airportthai.co.th.

## Airport Access

Don Mueang airport is across the highway from Don Mueang train station (accessible via an elevated walkway from the terminal). Trains travel to Bangkok's Hualamphong station roughly every hour or 1½ hours from 4am to 11.30am and then again every hour from 2pm to 9.30pm (3rd class ordinary/express 5/10B, one hour). Thanks to the new subway station at Hualamphong, final destinations in Silom and Sukhumvit are easier to reach than before.

It was uncertain at the time of writing if airport bus services would resume. A metered taxi trip from the airport into the middle of Bangkok should cost you around 200B to 300B, plus tolls (40B to 80B) and a 50B airport fee. Don't be shy in telling the driver to put the meter on.

As of writing, the only transport option between an international flight at Suvanabhumi and a domestic flight at Don Mueang is a taxi. Considering the vagaries of traffic, we would not recommend trying to make an international-domestic transfer in one day if your flight is departing from Don Mueang or vice versa.

## BUS

Government and private buses do trips from Bangkok to cities around Thailand, as well as to Malaysia. For long-distance trips, buses departing from the government bus terminals are more reliable and safer than buses leaving from tourist centres (such as Th Khao San).

**Northern & Northeastern bus terminal** ( ☎ for northern routes 2936 2852 ext 311, 442 for northeastern routes 0 2936 2852 ext 611, 448; Th Kamphaeng Phet) is just north of Chatuchak Park. It's also commonly called Mo Chit station. Buses depart from here for northern and northeastern destinations such as Chiang Mai and Ayuthaya. To reach the bus station, take Skytrain to Mo Chit and transfer onto city bus 512, 3, 49 or 77.

**Eastern bus terminal** ( ☎ 0 2391 2504; Soi 40/Soi Ekkamai, Th Sukhumvit) is the departure point for buses to Pattaya and Ban Phe, the boat pier to Ko Samet. Most people call it Ekkamai station. The Skytrain stops at its own Ekkamai station in front of Soi 63.

**Southern bus terminal** ( ☎ 0 2435 1200; Hwy 338/Th Nakhon Chaisi & Th Phra Pinkao, Thonburi) handles buses south to Phuket, Surat Thani and closer centres to the west such as Damnoen Saduak. This station is known as Sai Tai Mai and is in Thonburi. To reach the station, take bus 30 (for Banglamphu), 516 (for Thewet),

507 and 511 (for Pak Nam), 170 and 127 (for Mo Chit). Although there are plans to move the terminal further out of town, there is still no official word on when this will happen.

## TRAIN

From Hualamphong station, the main train station in Bangkok, there are five rail spurs – north to Chiang Mai, northeast to Nong Khai and Ubon Ratchathani (two lines that split at Khorat), southeast to Aranya Prathet (a border crossing-point to Cambodia) and south to Malaysia. Hualamphong has left-luggage facilities, although it is probably wiser to arrange this service at your hotel. In Thonburi, Bangkok Noi train station handles short-line routes to Kanchanaburi; there are no left-luggage facilities here.

To reserve seats call ☎ 0 2220 4444 or visit the advance booking office at Hualamphong. Trains come in three classes – from cattle car to comfy fold-out beds. The website www.seat61.com has helpful train-planning advice.

## TRAVEL DOCUMENTS
To enter Thailand, your passport must be valid for six months from the date of entry.

## VISAS
Residents of Australia, Canada, New Zealand, South Africa, the UK and the USA can stay in Bangkok for 30 days without a visa. If you plan on a longer trip, apply for a 60-day tourist visa or a 90-day non-immigrant visa before you leave home. You can also apply for a visa extension from the **Immigration Office** (Map p113, B6; ☎ 02 287 3101 10, Soi Suan Phlu, Th Sathon Tai); see the Ministry of Foreign Affairs website (www.mfa.go.th) for more information. Neighbouring countries also maintain embassies in Bangkok from which you can apply for a visa, but allow plenty of time.

## CLIMATE CHANGE & TRAVEL
Travel – especially air travel – is a significant contributor to global climate change. At Lonely Planet, we believe that all travellers have a responsibility to limit their personal impact. As a result, we have teamed with Rough Guides and other concerned industry partners to support Climate Care, which allows travellers to offset the greenhouse gases they are responsible for with contributions to energy-saving projects and other climate-friendly initiatives in the developing world. Lonely Planet offsets all staff and author travel.

For more information, turn to the responsible travel pages on www.lonelyplanet.com. For details on offsetting your carbon emissions and a carbon calculator, go to www.climatecare.org.

Do all visa applications and extensions in person rather than relying on a service to do it for you. Several travellers have been arrested prior to their departure from Thailand because of forged visa stamps acquired through agents.

### RETURN/ONWARD TICKET

Technically, you're supposed to demonstrate proof of a return or onward ticket; however, in practice, you are unlikely to be asked to show it.

### DEPARTURE TAX

International travellers have to pay a separate 700B departure tax after checking in at the airline counter.

....................................................

## GETTING AROUND

It can be tricky to decipher and pronounce Thailand's addresses. *Thànŏn* is a street, a *soi* is a laneway that runs off a *thànŏn* and a *trok* is an alley. In this book, 'Soi 6, Th Sukhumvit' means that Soi 6 runs off Th Sukhumvit. Building numbers often have confusing slashes and dashes, like 325/7-8 Th Charoen Krung. This stems from an old system of allocating property; the prefix in the address will be a helpful locator once you arrive on the street, but don't count on it as an indicator of the building's proximity to an intersection.

## BUS

The city's public bus system, which is operated by the Bangkok Metropolitan Transit Authority (BMTA), is the best option for reaching Chinatown, Banglamphu, Thewet, Dusit, and other areas not serviced by Skytrain. The buses are also a lot cheaper than the newer public transport options, but are also subject to the hassles of traffic. Air-con bus fares typically start at 10B or 12B and increase by increments of 2B, depending on the distance. Fares for ordinary buses (that come with a fan rather than air-con) start at 7B or 8B. Smaller 'baht buses' ply major *soi* and cost 5B.

The *Bangkok Bus Map* by Roadway, available at Asia Books (p83), is the most up-to-date route map available.

Hold on to your ticket as proof of purchase (an occasional formality).

## SKYTRAIN

The Skytrain (www.bts.co.th) has revolutionised travel around the newer districts of Bangkok. Trains arrive every few minutes from 6am to midnight. Tickets will cost you from 15B to 45B. Skytrain's one-day tourist pass (100B) is good for unlimited trips within a 24-hour period. Free shuttle buses on particular routes can drop you at Skytrain stations.

DIRECTORY

## Travel Around Bangkok

| | To Ko Ratanakosin | To Banglamphu | To Thewet and | To Chinatown |
|---|---|---|---|---|
| **From Ko Ratanakosin** | n/a | Ferry to Tha Phra Athit, Bus 53 | Ferry to Tha Thewet, Bus 53 | Ferry to Tha Ratcha |
| **From Banglamphu** | Ferry to Tha Chang, Bus 53 | n/a | Ferry to Tha Thewet, Bus 53 and 30 | Ferry to Tha Ratcha-wong, Bus 53 |
| **From Thewet and Dusit** | Ferry to Tha Chang, Bus 53 | Ferry to Tha Phra Athit, Bus 30 | n/a | Ferry to Tha Ratchawong |
| **From Chinatown** | Ferry to Tha Chang, Bus 53 | Ferry to Tha Phra Athit, Bus 53 | Ferry to Tha Thewet | n/a |
| **From Siam , Square Pratunam and Ploenchit** | Bus 508 and 59 | Bus 23 and 47; khlong taxi to Tha Phan Fah | Ferry to Tha Phra Athit, Bus 30 | Bus 73 |
| **From Silom and Riverside** | Ferry to Tha Chang | Ferry to Tha Phra Athit | Ferry to Tha Thewet | Ferry to Tha Ratcha wong; Silom subway station to Hualamphong |
| **From Lumphini** | Skytrain from Sala transfer to ferry at Tha Daeng to Saphan Taksin, Sathon to Tha Chang | Skytrain from Sala transfer to ferry at Tha to Saphan Taksin, Sathon to Tha Phra Athit | Skytrain from Sala transfer to ferry at Tha Daeng to Saphan , Taksin Sathon to Tha Thewet | Subway from LumphinIto Hualamphong |
| **From Th Sukhumvit** | Skytrain to National Stadium, transfer to Bus 508 | Skytrain to National Stadium, transfer to Bus 47 | Skytrain to Ratchath-,ewi transfer to Bus 2 | Subway from Sukhumvit to Hualamphong |

Ticket machines at each station accept 5B and 10B coins only, but change is available from the staffed information booths. You can also buy value-stored tickets and pick up brochures detailing the various commuter and tourist passes at the info booths.

| Siam Square, Pratunam Dusit | Silom and Riverside | Lumphini and Ploenchit | Th Sukhumvit |
| --- | --- | --- | --- |
| Bus 508, transfer at National Stadium Skytrain for Ploenchit; Bus 59 for Pratunam | Ferry to Tha Sathon, transfer at Saphan Taksin Skytrain to Sala | Ferry to Tha Sathon, transfer at Saphan Taksin Skytrain to Sala Daeng | Bus 508, transfer to National Stadium Skytrain to desired station |
| Bus 23 and 47, transfer at National Stadium Skytrain for Ploenchit; khlong taxi to Pratunam | Ferry to Tha Sathon, transfer at Saphan Taksin Skytrain to Sala Daeng | Ferry to Tha Sathon, transfer at Saphan Taksin Skytrain to Sala Daeng | Bus 47, transfer to National Stadium Skytrain to desired station; or khlong taxi to nearest pier |
| Bus 47, transfer at National Stadium Skytrain for Ploenchit; Bus 23 to Pratunam | Ferry to Tha Sathon, Skytrain transfer at Saphan Taksin to Sala Daeng | Ferry to Tha Sathon, transfer at Saphan Taksin Skytrain to Sala Daeng | Bus 2, transfer to Ratchathewi Skytrain to desired station |
| Bus 73, transfer at National Stadium Skytrain for Ploenchit | Ferry to Tha Sathon, transfer at Saphan Taksin Skytrain to Sala Daeng; Hualamphong subway to Silom | Ferry to Tha Sathon, transfer at Saphan Taksin Skytrain to Sala Daeng or Hualamphong subway to Lumphini | Hualamphong subway to Silom, transfer at Sala Daeng Skytrain |
| n/a | Skytrain to Sala Daeng or Chong Nonsi | Skytrain to Sala Daeng, Ploenchit or transfer from Sala Daeng Skytrain to Lumphini | Skytrain to desired station |
| Skytrain to desired station | n/a | Subway to Lumphini | Skytrain to desired station |
| Skytrain from Sala Daeng to desired station | Subway from Lumphini to Silom | n/a | Skytrain from Sala Daeng to desired station or Skytrain from Lumphini to Sukhumvit |
| Skytrain to desired station | Skytrain or subway from Sukhumvit to Silom | Subway from Sukhumvit to Lumphini | n/a |

Once through the ticket gates, follow the signs for the desired line and terminus you can transfer between the two lines at the Siam interchange station. The Sukhumvit line terminates in the north of the city at the Mo Chit station, next to Chatuchak Park, and follows Th Phayathai south to Siam interchange station at Th Rama I and then swings east along Th Ploenchit and Th Sukhumvit to terminate at the On Nut station, near Soi 81. There are plans to extend this line 5km southeast to Soi 107, Th Sukhumvit.

The Silom line runs from the National Stadium station, near Siam Square, and soon after makes an abrupt turn to the southwest, continuing above Th Ratchadamri, down Th Silom to Th Narathiwat Ratchanakharin, then out Th Sathon until it terminates next to the foot of Saphan Taksin on the banks of Mae Nam Chao Phraya. There are plans to extend this line a further 4.5km over the river into Thonburi.

## SUBWAY

The first line of Bangkok's subway opened in 2004 and connects the railway station of Bang Sue with the following interchange stations connecting to the Skytrain stops: Chatuchak Park (Mo Chit Skytrain station), Sukhumvit (Asoke Skytrain station), and Silom (Sala Daeng Skytrain station) and terminating at Hualamphong. Trains operate from 5am to midnight and cost 14B to 36B, depending on distance. Future extensions will connect Hualamphong to Chinatown and Thonburi.

For short-term visitors, the subway makes Hualamphong station and the convention centre easier to reach from Silom and Sukhumvit.

## BOAT

For sights in Banglamphu, Ko Ratanakosin and some parts of Silom, the **Chao Phraya Express Boat** ( ☎ 0 2623 6001, ext 101; www.chaophraya boat.co.th) is the most convenient option. The service runs from 6am to 7.30pm; you can buy tickets (8B to 27B) on board. Boats with yellow or red-and-orange flags are express boats. These boats run during peak times and therefore don't make every stop. A **tourist boat** ( ⏳ 9.30am-4pm) runs from Tha Sathon (Map pp140–141, B8) with stops at 10 major sightseeing piers; a 100B unlimited day-pass is also available. Hold on to your ticket as proof of purchase (an occasional formality).

Longtail khlong taxis zip around Bangkok's Khlong Saen Saeb, conducting quick trips from Tha Withayu (Map p81, E1), Tha Pratunam (Map p81, D1) and Tha Ratchathewi (Map p81, A1) to Tha Phan Fah (near Wat Saket; Map p55, E3). Fares cost from 5B to 8B and it runs from 6am to 7pm.

At all boat piers, private longtail boats can be hired for sightseeing trips.

## TAXI

Taxis in Bangkok are plentiful but victims of traffic vagaries. Always take meter taxis and insist on using the meters. Don't take taxis that quote a price (typically three times higher than the metered price). You pay a 35B flag fall, then 4.5B per kilometre for trips between 2km and 12km, 5B per kilometre between 13km and 20km and 5.5B per kilometre for more than 20km; in a traffic jam you pay 1.25B a minute. You pay a 50B surcharge for trips leaving the airport and all tolls. There is talk of increasing the flag fall to 40B. Report complaints to ☎ 0 2272 5460.

## TÚK-TÚK

These putt-putting three-wheeled vehicles are tourist-traps – they'll zip you to an overpriced tailor or jeweller regardless of your destination. For kicks, take them for short hops (within a neighbourhood); 40B is usually a fair price. Refuse to enter any unrequested shop. Skip the 10B sightseeing offers.

## MOTORCYCLE TAXI

Need to be somewhere in a hurry during rush hour? A jaunt on a motorcycle taxi is guaranteed to be super-quick and (hopefully) death-defying. Rides from the main road to the end of a *soi* is usually 10B. Women wearing skirts should ride side-saddle.

## CAR & MOTORCYCLE

You're either extremely patient or mad to drive in Bangkok. Even once you get somewhere, parking is usually a nightmare. You are required to have an International Driving Permit to drive in Bangkok. You'll pay around 28B/L for petrol.

Appearances may be deceiving, but there are road rules in Bangkok.

Car hire starts at around 1800B per day, but the rate often gets cheaper if you hire by the week or month. Rental companies include **Avis** (Map p81, E3; ☎ 0 2255 5300; 2/12 Th Withayu; ⏰ 8am-6pm) and other international franchises.

If your car breaks down, you could try getting in touch with **Carworld Club** ( ☎ 0 2612 9999), which offers roadside assistance.

# PRACTICALITIES
## BUSINESS HOURS

Bangkok is predominantly an on-the-go, seven-days-a-week town. Restaurants generally open from around 10am to 10pm, shops from 10am to 8pm. Businesses along Th Charoen Krung close on Sunday. Most government offices are open from 8.30am to 4.30pm weekdays. Some government offices close from noon to 1pm for lunch, while others have Saturday hours (9am-3pm). Banking hours are typically 8.30am to 3.30pm Monday to Friday.

## ELECTRICITY

Electric currents in Thailand are 220V, 50 cycles. Most electrical wall outlets take the round, two-prong terminals, but some will take flat, two-bladed terminals and others will take both. Converters can be easily bought from electrical stores throughout the city.

## HOLIDAYS

Lunar holidays change each year; for detailed information, check out the **TAT website** (www.tatnews.org).
**New Year's Day** 1 January
**Magha Puja (lunar)** January-March
**Chakri Day** 6 April
**Songkhran Festival (lunar)** April
**Coronation Day** 5 May
**Visakha Puja (lunar)** May
**Asalha Puja (lunar)** July
**Khao Phansa (lunar)** July
**Queen's Birthday** 12 August
**Chulalongkorn Day** 23 October
**King's Birthday** 5 December
**Constitution Day** 10 December

## INTERNET

Internet access is widely available at internet cafés, costing anywhere from 40B to 150B per hour; wi-fi access at internet cafés is becoming more widespread. High-end hotels have wi-fi in the lobby and either wi-fi or broadband in the rooms for an extra daily charge. Tamarind Café (p133) offers free wi-fi access.
**2 Bangkok** www.2bangkok.com

**Lonely Planet** www.lonelyplanet.com
**Bangkok Tourist Division** www.bangkoktourist.com
**Bangkok Post** www.bangkokpost.net
**The Nation** www.nationmultimedia.com
**Tourism Authority of Thailand** www.tat.or.th

## LANGUAGE

Thailand's official language is Thai. The dialect from Central Thailand has been adopted as the lingua franca, though regional dialects are still spoken. Thai is a tonal language, with five tones. Written Thai is read from left to right. Transliteration of Thai into the roman alphabet renders multiple (and contradictory) spellings. After every sentence, men affix the polite particle *kháp*, and women *khá*.

### BASICS

| | |
|---|---|
| Hello. | *sà wàt dii* |
| How are you? | *sa·bai dii rěu?* |
| I'm fine. | *sa·bai dii* |
| Excuse me. | *khǎw thôht* |
| Yes. | *châi* |
| No. | *mâi châi* |
| Thank you. | *khàwp khun* |
| You're welcome. | *mâi pen rai* |
| Do you speak English? | *phûut phaa-sǎa ang-krìt dâi mǎi?* |
| I don't understand. | *mâi khâo jai* |
| How much is this? | *nîi thâo rai?* |
| That's too expensive. | *phaeng koen pai* |

## EATING & DRINKING

| | |
|---|---|
| That was delicious! | khàwp khun mâak, aràwy mâak |
| Please bring the bill. | khaw bin |
| I'm allergic to … | phŏm/dì-chan pháe … |
| I don't eat … | phŏm/dì-chan kin … mâi dâi |
| meat | néua sàt |
| chicken | kài |
| fish | plaa |

Here are some common local dishes that you'll most likely come across:

kaeng khĭaw-wăan kài – green curry with chicken; usually not very spicy

kaeng phèt kài/néua/mŭu – red curry with chicken/beef/pork; very spicy

kŭaytĭaw lûuk chin mŭu – noodle soup with pork balls

phàt thai – thin rice noodles fried with tofu, vegetables, egg & peanuts

tôm yam kûng – prawn & lemon grass soup with mushrooms

## EMERGENCIES

| | |
|---|---|
| I'm sick. | chăn pùay |
| Help! | chûay dûay! |
| Call a doctor! | rîak măw nàwy! |
| Call the police! | rîak tam·rùat nàwy! |

## TIME & NUMBERS

| | |
|---|---|
| today | wan níi |
| tomorrow | phrûng níi |
| yesterday | mêua waan |

| | |
|---|---|
| 0 | sŭun |
| 1 | nèung |
| 2 | săwng |
| 3 | săam |
| 4 | sìi |
| 5 | hâa |
| 6 | hòk |
| 7 | jèt |
| 8 | pàet |
| 9 | kâo |
| 10 | sìp |
| 11 | sìp-èt |
| 12 | sìp-săwng |
| 13 | sìp-săam |
| 20 | yîi-sìp |
| 21 | yîi-sìp-èt |
| 22 | yîi-sìp-săwng |
| 30 | săam-sìp |
| 100 | nèung ráwy |
| 200 | săwng ráwy |
| 1000 | nèung phan |

## MONEY

### CURRENCY

The basic unit of Thai currency is the baht (B), made up of 100 satang. Notes come in 20B, 50B, 100B, 500B and 1000B. Coins come in 1B, 5B, 10B and occasionally 25 or 50 satang. Go to 7-Eleven shops or hotels to break 1000B notes; don't expect a vendor/taxi to have change for 500B or anything larger.

DIRECTORY

## TRAVELLERS CHEQUES

Travellers cheques are easily cashed for a commission at major banks in Bangkok. Buy cheques in US dollars or British pounds to avoid possible hassles.

## CREDIT CARDS

You'll have few problems using your credit card – especially if it's a Visa, MasterCard, Diners Club or Amex – at most higher-end hotels and restaurants. For 24-hour card cancellations or assistance, call:

**American Express** (☎ 0 2273 5544)
**Diners Club** (☎ 0 2238 3660)
**MasterCard** (☎ 001 800 11887 0663)
**Visa** (☎ 001 800 11535 0660)

## ATMS

Automatic Teller Machines are widespread and usually accept Cirrus, Plus, Maestro, JCB and Visa cards.

## CHANGING MONEY

The banks offer the best rates for changing money. They're generally open from 8.30am to 3.30pm Monday to Friday but some have currency exchange counters that operate from 8am to 8pm.

## NEWSPAPERS & MAGAZINES

Bangkok has two English-language broadsheets: *Bangkok Post* and The *Nation*. Visit Asia Books (p83) and Kinokuniya (p84) for English-language material.

## PHOTOGRAPHY & VIDEO

Print and slide film and VHS video cassettes are widely available and inexpensive. There are many film-processing labs, with good rates, throughout the city. Thailand uses the PAL video system, which is compatible with Europe (except France) and Australia. Some video shops sell NTSC format tapes, compatible with the USA and Japan. Most internet cafés are equipped to transfer digital photographs to CD.

## TELEPHONE

Phone booths are widespread and well-marked as being local or international, phone card- or change-accepting. Phone booths in shopping centres will be quieter than streetside. Phone cards are widely available and will cost you 100B for domestic and 300B for international cards. You can buy handsets and SIM cards at Mah Boon Krong (p24). Or arrange global roaming for your mobile phone before you get to Bangkok.

## COUNTRY & CITY CODES

All Thai phone numbers now have eight digits. Mobile phone numbers now have an '8' prefix;

phone numbers beginning with 01, 04, 06, 09 will become 081, 084, 086, 089.

**Thailand** ☎ 66
**Bangkok (land lines)** ☎ 02

## USEFUL NUMBERS
**Local Directory Inquiries** ☎ 1133
**International Operator** ☎ 100
**Reverse-Charge (collect)** ☎ 100

## INTERNATIONAL DIRECT DIAL CODES
Dial ☎ 001, 008 or 007 followed by:

**Australia** ☎ 61
**Canada** ☎ 1
**Japan** ☎ 81
**New Zealand** ☎ 64
**South Africa** ☎ 27
**UK** ☎ 44
**USA** ☎ 1

## TIPPING
Tipping practices vary in Thailand, but many midrange and expensive restaurants add a 10% service charge to the bill in addition to a 7% VAT (value-added tax).

## TOURIST INFORMATION
### TOURIST INFORMATION ABROAD
**Australia & New Zealand** ( ☎ 02 9247 7549; 2nd fl, 75 Pitt St, Sydney, NSW 2000)
**Singapore** ( ☎ 56 235 7901; c/o Royal Thai Embassy, 370 Orchard Rd, Singapore 238870)
**UK** ( ☎ 07 925 2511; 3rd fl, Brook House, 98-99 Jermyn St, London SW1Y 6EE)

**USA & Canada** ( ☎ 323-461-9814; 611 N Larchmont Blvd, 1st fl, Los Angeles, CA 90004; ☎ 212-432-0433; 61 Broadway, Suite 2810; New York, NY 10006)

## LOCAL TOURIST INFORMATION
Beware of bogus tourist offices or officials purporting to be the real deal. The organisations below do not make travel arrangements.
**Bangkok Tourist Division** (Map p55, A2; ☎ 0 2225 7612-5; 17/1 Th Phra Athit; ⏱ 9am-7pm) also has yellow information booths throughout the city.
**Tourism Authority of Thailand Information Office** (TAT; Map p55, E2; ☎ 0 2283 1555; cnr Th Ratchadamnoen Nok & Th Chakrapatdipong; ⏱ 8.30am-4.30pm)
**Tourist Police** (Map pp122-3, C1; ☎ 1155; CMIC Tower, 209/1 Soi Asoke, Th Sukhumvit; ⏱ 24hr) for reporting crimes.

## TRAVELLING WITH DISABILITIES
Movement around the streets of Bangkok can be a complete nightmare for someone with impaired mobility – there are few sloping kerbs or wheelchair ramps, and many streets are best crossed via stair-heavy pedestrian crossings. Some disabled travellers hire a taxi or a private car and driver to see the sights, rather than taking tours, although it can be difficult to fit a wheelchair in the taxi boot. Five Skytrain stations have lifts: Asoke, Chong Nonsi, Mo Chit, On

Nut and Siam Square. You can travel for free from these stations if you show your disabled association membership. Some hotel chains, like Amari and Banyan Tree, are particularly aware of the needs of disabled travellers.

This book indicates disabled accessibility with the following ratings: excellent (compliant with international accessibility access), good (elevator, easy street access), fair (steps, narrow passageways, no elevator).

## INFORMATION & ORGANISATIONS
**Gimp on the Go** (www.gimponthego.com)
**Society for Accessible Travel & Hospitality** (www.sath.org)

# >INDEX

*See also separate subindexes for See (p212), Shop (p213), Eat (p214), Drink (p215) and Play (p215).*

## ⦿ SEE